CALLING FATHERS TO ARISE!

Knowing God As Father
and Becoming a *Godly*
and *Spiritual* Father Like Him

DR. JAMES RENE

CALLING FATHERS TO ARISE!

To contact the author about speaking at your conference or church, please go to www.jamesreneministries.com

Scripture quotations from the Holy Bible, English Standard Version®, (ESV), Copyright © 2001 by Crossway, a publishing ministry of Good News Publishers. Used by permission. All rights reserved.

The Holy Bible, New International Version®, (NIV), Copyright © 1973, 1978, 1984, 2011 by Biblica. Inc.™ Used by permission. All rights reserved worldwide.

Scripture taken from the New King James Version®, (NKJV), Copyright © 1982 by Thomas Nelson, Inc. Used by permission. All rights reserved.

Scripture taken from the New American Standard®, (NASB), Copyright © 1960, 1962, 1963, 1968, 1971, 1973, 1975, 1977, 1995, by The Lockman Foundation. Used by permission.

Scripture quotations marked (NLT) are taken from the Holy Bible, New Living Translation, Copyright © 1996, 2004, 2007 by Tyndale House foundation. Used by permission of Tyndale House Publishers, Inc. All rights reserved.

Scripture quotations marked (TPT) are from The Passion Translation®, Copyright © 2017, 2017 by Passion & Fire Ministries, Inc. Used by permission. All rights reserved.

Scripture quotations taken from the Amplified® Bible (AMP), Copyright © 2015 by The Lockman Foundation. Used by permission.

Scripture quotations marked (CEV) are from the Contemporary English Version, Copyright © 1991, 1992, 1995 by American Bible Society. Used by permission.

Scripture quotations taken from the Holy Bible, New International Readers Version®, (NIrV), Copyright © 1996, 1998, Biblica. Used by permission. All rights reserved.

Paperback ISBN 978-1-7357486-0-3
Hardback ISBN 978-1-7357486-1-0
eBook ISBN 978-1-7357486-2-7

ENDORSEMENTS

"My friend, James Rene, has done a tremendous job in his very timely book. In *Calling Fathers to Arise!*, he goes beyond just a cursory study on the topic of fathers and prophetically calls us out, and up. With decades of ministerial experience and a genuine father's heart, James is beyond an idealist; he is a true practitioner of what he is writing."

—Johnny Enlow
Author, International Speaker & Prophetic Leader (www.Restore7.org)

"Calling Fathers to Arise! by Dr. James Rene is one of the most well-written masterpieces on spiritual fathering. It is a must-read for anyone considering to deepen their knowledge on the subject of godly and spiritual fathering. This book comes from a man whom I personally know as one of the best fathers to his own family, as well as to spiritual sons and daughters around the world."

—Dr. Charles Karuku
Senior Pastor I.O.C, Burnsville MN &
President of Institute of Leadership and Mentorship

"In his book, *Calling Fathers to Arise!*, my dear friend, James Rene, explores the fatherhood of God for generational legacy. While living through the absence of a biological father, James Rene is uniquely prepared to inspire fatherhood. He does so without promulgating any sense of low-grade guilt that sometimes comes through such introspective books. *Calling Fathers to Arise!* is a must-read for those who seek to live the heart of Father God, and see the next generations as valuable for eternity."

—Dr. Wayman Ming Jr.

Presiding Bishop of the Pentecostal Church of God

"In *Calling Fathers to Arise!: Knowing God As Father And Becoming a Godly and Spiritual Father Like Him,* Dr. James Rene has produced a book that will resonate with many and prophetically communicate the Father's heart for the Church today. The book is insightful, well-researched, transparent, prophetic and is delivered from the heart of a spiritual father. I would strongly commend this timely book for those who understand that the people of God need more than church programs and serving opportunities. They long for deep and meaningful relationships, especially the spiritual and apostolic fathers."

—Dr. Rolo Santos

Executive Pastor, Water of Life Community Church, Fontana CA

"I'm not just proud of my friend's accomplishment in completing the book in your hands; I'm impacted and inspired. Spiritual parenting, like parenting in the natural, requires work and time investment. James captures not only the *why* for spiritual parenting, but offers the *how to* in very practical ways that will help guide anyone who values the relationship between spiritual parents and children. James has traveled the world and has first-hand experience in witnessing the principles written herein play out in diverse cultures and nations. I highly recommend this book!"

—Jeff Kenney

Destiny Fellowship of Churches & Ministries, West Coast Director

DEDICATION

This book is, first and foremost, dedicated to my Heavenly Father. Thank You for rescuing me, choosing me, and giving me life and purpose as Your loving son and minister of the Gospel. You truly are a Father to the fatherless. This book is for Your honor and glory.

Secondly, I dedicate this book to my beautiful wife, Laura, whose incredible love, care, and support to me as a husband, father, pastor, and international minister has meant the world to me. She has been my source of strength, inspiration, and perseverance in my life and ministry. She is truly God's greatest gift to me. None can compare with her.

To my sons, I love you with all my heart. I am so proud of the young men you have become. You continue to challenge and inspire me to become the best father that I can be.

ACKNOWLEDGEMENTS

I would like to express my heartfelt gratitude and thanks to Tony Hart, who has been a spiritual father and dear friend to me for the past twelve years. Your continual encouragement and cheering me on in my calling and ministry have been invaluable in my life. Thanks for taking the time to listen as I read each chapter to you. I'm grateful to God for your input, enthusiastic support, and belief in the message of *Calling Fathers to Arise!*

To my brilliant niece, Sarah Howell, you did an amazing job as my editor. Thank you for partnering with me in this writing project. You've added an incredible personal touch and writing excellence that I could not have produced on my own.

To my sister, Nancy Washack, thanks for your love and prayers for my family and me, and for being an amazing support to God's calling upon my life. Thanks for listening and reading the drafts of the chapters of my book. Your input as a former English teacher was a lot of fun.

To my brother, David Gomez, thanks for partnering with me with *James Rene Ministries* to get the message of the Gospel and my ministry training resources out to the world. Let's keep it going to make a difference for Jesus!

To my friend, Jeff Kenny, thanks for your support, encouragement, and input on my chapters. You've helped me tremendously! You are an amazing spiritual father to God's family.

Lastly, but most importantly, to my mother, Virginia Umana, thank you for your unconditional love, support, and prayers for me throughout my life. They have lifted and carried me more than you'll ever know. I love you with all my heart.

CONTENTS

ENDORSEMENTS III

DEDICATION..V

ACKNOWLEDGEMENTS VII

FOREWORD XI

INTRODUCTION...XIII

CHAPTER 1   THE GLOBAL EPIDEMIC AND
             CONSEQUENCES OF FATHERLESSNESS.................1

CHAPTER 2   "SHOW US THE FATHER"....................................15

CHAPTER 3   THE FATHERHOOD OF GOD 35

CHAPTER 4   BECOMING A SON OF GOD TO BECOME A
             GODLY FATHER...51

CHAPTER 5   THE CALL AND ROLE OF GODLY
             FATHERS IN THE HOME 65

CHAPTER 6   THE CALL AND ROLE OF SPIRITUAL
             FATHERS IN THE CHURCH..............................93

CHAPTER 7   THE CALL AND ROLE OF MODERN
             APOSTOLIC FATHERS 129

A CLOSING WORD OF ENCOURAGEMENT 141

ENDNOTES 143

FOREWORD

Dr. James Rene has earned the title as one of the leading Global Voices in fathering in our modern times. The power of this book is given to us by Dr. Rene in real-time, at every level of fathering. His knowledge and research on this subject are so extensive that he must be considered the head of the class.

I have personally traveled to eighty nations of the World and have met numerous World Leaders, as well as spiritual leaders, and I can truly say I have never found any book or literature as impactful on the subject of fathering as this book. I personally classify Dr. James Rene as a leading voice in the present-day truth in the conversation of fathering around the world.

What makes this more impactful for me is that I have known Dr. James Rene for over twenty years, and his life matches his message. Every institution of impact that wants to build a better future for us all needs to implement the study of this book to build solid foundations for our world and future generations. I was truly humbled to be asked to write the foreword for this amazing man and world leader.

Sir Clyde Rivers
World Civility Leader

INTRODUCTION

THE CRY OF THE FATHERLESS

A young man is sitting in church on Sunday, Bible in hand, third row, per usual. Families sit all around him, dressed in their best, one in matching L.A. Lakers jerseys, one with a young child, another in what appears to be grandparents and children, three generations, all in a row. It's Father's Day, and this young man is sitting all alone. The pastor is showing, on the main screen, some of the cards his own kids wrote to him that year. The whole congregation is laughing at his daughter's note making fun of his tie collection. The sermon after is all about respecting elders and how to learn from your father. The dad in front of him nudges his teenage son a little. The young man questions why he even came to church that day; this sermon doesn't apply to him. It's not the fault of the families around him for spending extra time with their own dads and granddads that day. It's not the pastor's fault for trying to honor the fathers in the room. It's not even his own fault that he was raised without a dad leaving him with a huge void and cry in his heart wishing he had known and belonged to a father.

Calling Fathers to Arise! was borne out of my heart's cry and burden to see the fatherless in our nation and around the world come to know the love of Father God and to be restored to wholeness to fulfill their life's calling and purpose. When I speak of the fatherless, I'm not just speaking of those who are without natural fathers, but also those who have fathers who are absent, distant, or alienated from them.

This cry and burden began with my own personal experience of not having a father for most of my life. I had an adopted father from the age of five to fifteen, whom I believed was my biological father. At age fifteen, during a period where we seemed to never get along, I discovered he was not my biological father and that I had been adopted by him. This revelation sent me into a tailspin that caused an immediate identity crisis for me. Who am I? Was everything I was told growing up a lie? What happened to my biological father? As a result of this shock and confusion, I was overwhelmed, which compelled me to run away from home. I began to battle with who I was because of it, and this identity crisis only grew. As a result of my realization that my assumed father, who was raising me, was not my biological father, and me running away, he completely rejected me. Several years later, he divorced my mother.

The outcome of these traumatic events has resulted in me spending over forty years of my life without a father. This impacted my life deeply on many fronts, for decades. But by God's grace, I discovered and received Christ as my savior at age twenty-six, and He took me through a process over the years where I found healing, transformation, and purpose through the love of my Heavenly Father. My personal experience with being fatherless has given me tremendous understanding, great love, compassion, and a burden for the fatherless. A burden to see the fatherless saved, healed, restored, and transformed by the love of Father God, who is a Father to the fatherless.

In addition to my personal experience, God's calling upon my life as a five-fold minister to the nations has shown me how prevalent the problem and tragic consequences of fatherlessness is around the world. God has taken me to twenty-three nations in the past twenty years, where I've seen, firsthand, the massive problem and impact of fatherlessness across the world. I've seen the huge void of fathers and godly fatherhood, not only in our homes, but also in the void of spiritual and apostolic fatherhood in our churches and communities. Divorce, broken homes, absent, distant or abusive fathers, distorted family structures, alternative families, false religions, humanistic godless cultures, disease, wars, human tragedies—all of these things combined over the decades, have produced a "natural" and spiritual fatherless generation.

Religious Church systems with controlling or self-serving denominational and pastoral church leadership have produced a spiritual fatherless generation in our churches. The results of these voids are: wounded sons and daughters not becoming all that God has created them to be; a multiplication of dysfunctional fatherhood, broken families and communities, and unfulfilled destinies; cities and nations are being discipled by the spirit of this world and led by ungodly, corrupt, or self-serving leadership; churches are being greatly limited in the building and maturing of the body of Christ, equipping and maturing of God's sons and daughters, and in Christ's mission of discipling the nations. Unless godly, spiritual, and apostolic fathers arise and function as God intends, the fatherless cycle and the generational and societal consequences will continue!

This book is written from this burden and cry of the fatherless to provide some understanding and truth of our Heavenly Father's heart, burden, and call for godly and spiritual fathers to arise. It is my hope and prayer that this book will contribute toward the needed transformational change. The chapters will reveal biblical truth and practical insight into the Fatherhood of God and the role of godly, spiritual, and modern apostolic fathers to father and equip sons and daughters for life and their kingdom calling.

It will reveal that the Fatherhood of God, as expressed through these fathers, is God's design, order, and a key source for equipping and maturing natural and spiritual sons and daughters. It is the cornerstone for building godly families and establishing and multiplying strong apostolic churches to transform their communities, cities, and nation.

The message of this book is mostly for fathers. However, I believe it will also bring hope and healing to both men and women who have been wounded by hurtful or absent relationships with their earthly fathers. My hope and prayer is that it will help you to see God's heart for you in a deeper way, and draw you to develop a closer, more intimate relationship with Him as your Heavenly Father.

—James Rene

1

THE GLOBAL EPIDEMIC AND CONSEQUENCES OF FATHERLESSNESS

As I shared in my introduction, God has taken me around the world to twenty-three nations. I've served on over fifty missions to preach the Gospel to the unsaved and to equip God's people for the work of the ministry. The majority of my international missions and ministry have been to the nations of Africa. I'll never forget the time I was in Nairobi, Kenya, several years ago. I could not help but notice young women, together with older foreign men, everywhere at the coffee shops, cafes, restaurants, malls, walking down the street, airport, etc. I was struck by the prevalence of what I was seeing and had to ask my Kenyan pastor friend, who was with me, why this was. I asked him if these young women were dating or married to these older foreign men to receive security, care, and provision. I asked, "Was this prostitution in some cases? Is this the result of some void in their lives?" His answer to me was, he believed, "It was due to the void and hunger for love, care, and security they long for because of not having a relationship with a father."

I'll never forget that time in Kenya, as it was the straw that broke the camel's back and the catalyst to compel me to write about the cry of the fatherless and void of godly fathers around the world. The prayer within my heart at that moment was for Father God to anoint me to write from His heart with a message to call godly fathers to arise. For God to anoint me by His Spirit to produce a tool to equip godly and spiritual fathers across the nations. I prayed in my heart that this would be a resource that I could provide to God's ministers and people, wherever God sends me to serve, that will make a difference! My Kenyan friend told me, "God has commissioned you on this mission to write on this. This will be one of the books you will write. It's time for you to start writing." That moment in Kenya has never left me, and by God's divine providence, several years later, that particular book is what you are now reading.

Kenya is just one of many nations that has a significant number of children and youth growing up without a father in the home. 22% of children in Kenya live with their mothers, while their fathers are alive and live elsewhere. The death of a father only accounts for 5.3% of the households.[1]

According to the Organization for Economic Co-operation and Development, 17% of children live in single-parent households worldwide, and 88% of these households are headed up by women. Denmark, the United Kingdom, Lithuania and the United States have the highest percentage of single mother households from 23% to 26%.[2]

Over 60% of South African kids are in homes without fathers. 10% of these households have lost their fathers due to death, while 50% of the fathers are alive but are not present in the lives of their kids.[3]

In a Pew Research Center study of 130 countries, it showed that the U.S. has the world's highest rate of children living in single-parent households.[4] As many as 25% of children in the U.S. live in households with a mother alone.[5] An estimated 24.7 million children live absent of their biological fathers.[6]

For those of us who live in America, think about these statistics for a moment. We are the most prosperous nation in the world. We are the most prosperous generation that has ever lived. Yet, we have the highest rate of single-parent households and one of the highest rates of fatherless children in the world. Are we really a prosperous nation? What then does it mean to be truly prosperous? Is it material wealth and the things of this world, or is true prosperity the strength and multiplication of godly families that establish godly communities, cities, and nations? *What do we profit if we gain the whole world, but lose our soul?* A nation is only as great as its fathers.

Another statistic that reveals the magnitude of fatherlessness globally is the data concerning orphans. UNICEF reported in 2015 that there were nearly 140 million orphans worldwide, 61 million in Asia, 52 million in Africa, 10 million in Latin America and the Caribbean, and 7.3 million in Eastern Europe and Central Asia. These figures represent not only children who have lost both parents, but also those who have lost a father.[7]

The sampling of the global numbers of the fatherless I've presented above is staggering. And yet, they are still merely a sample of the extent of this issue. We could look deeper, look into country by country statistics, look into those who live in homes with abusive fathers, those that are reported. Nonetheless, it is overwhelming. The data over the decades reveals that this problem is multiplying by leaps and bounds each decade. And if we do not reverse the course, an absentee father society will become a permanent reality in America and many other nations of the world.

More than ever, do we need God's Spirit to be poured upon us and the Word of the Lord, through the prophet Malachi to *"turn the hearts of the Fathers"* to come to pass? *"Behold, I will send you Elijah the prophet before the coming of the great and dreadful day of the* LORD. *And he will turn the hearts of the fathers to the children, and the hearts of the children to their fathers, lest I come and strike the earth with a curse"* Malachi 4:4-6 (NKJV).

Fatherlessness is truly one of the most troubling social ills in our world, and the impact it is having on individuals and societies across the nations are truly characteristics of the curse. Here are some of the tragic consequences of fatherlessness in America:

- Fatherless children are at a dramatically greater risk of drug and alcohol abuse, mental illness, suicide, poor educational performance, teen pregnancy, and criminality (U.S. Dept. of Health and Human Services, National Center for Health Statistics).
- 90% of homeless and runaway children are from fatherless homes (U.S. Dept. of Health and Human Services, Census Bureau).
- 85% of all children who exhibit behavioral disorders come from fatherless homes (CDC).
- 63% of youth suicides are from fatherless homes (U.S. Dept. of Health and Human Services).
- 71% of all high school dropouts come from a fatherless home (National Principals Association Report on the State of High Schools).

- 85% of youth in prisons grew up in a fatherless home (Texas Department of Corrections).
- 75% of prisoners grew up in a fatherless home (D. Amneus, *The Garbage Generation*).
- 80% of rapists motivated with displaced anger come from fatherless homes (Criminal Justice and Behavior Report, Vol. 14).
- 71% of pregnant teenagers lack a father (U.S. Dept. of Health and Human Services).
- Daughters of single parents without a father are 53% more likely to marry as teenagers, 711% more likely to have children as teenagers, 164% likely to have a pre-marital birth, and 92% more likely to get divorced (Statistics: The Fatherless Generation wordpress.com).
- Children with a weak or absent relationship with their father are 68% more likely to smoke, drink, or use drugs compared to teens in two-parent households (Columbia University Research).

The tragic consequences of fatherlessness that I've listed do not cover all of the issues that exist. These consequences do not only exist in America; they are taking place globally. Percentages may vary, and there are other issues depending on the country, culture, and city where one lives, but the overall impact of fatherlessness is the same.

FATHERLESS DAUGHTERS

Many teenage girls around the world are suffering from emotional trauma as a result of being fatherless. The loss of a father caused by divorce, physical or emotional absence, abandonment, addiction, imprisonment, death, etc., whatever the circumstances, has a severe and life-altering impact, as the father-daughter relationship strongly influences their personal development in relationships, self-esteem, life aspirations, confidence, and self-love.

As they grow older, they can become vulnerable young women who find it harder to build healthy personal and professional lives. This is because they are building their lives, relationships, life aspirations, and self-presentation on the basis of this trauma, especially when it occurs during adolescence. They can suffer from trust issues, low self-esteem, and fear of abandonment, which create an unhealthy need to be accepted and loved at all costs.[8]

Fatherless young women can often become self-destructive, vulnerable, sexually promiscuous, prone to abuse, unstable, and develop a conflicted relationship with their femininity and sexuality. Many struggle to trust because of a deep-rooted fear of abandonment. This leads them down a desperate road, constantly seeking the approval of others. Romantic relationships are undoubtedly the area in which the impact of a father's loss is felt the most in a young woman's life. Many find themselves in unhealthy and often abusive relationships after idealizing this illusory father figure they never had and would have loved to have, and allowed it to influence their choice in a partner. It is common that fatherless young women unconsciously repeat the same relationship patterns that manifest through a constant fear of abandonment, insecurities, difficulties to open up, a conflictual relationship to male authority, and defense mechanisms. They usually create a shell around themselves that seems strong on the outside, but deep inside, they remain extremely vulnerable.[9]

A daughter without a father is not worthless; she is not hopeless; she is not purposeless. In many ways, she can become stronger, more resilient, more determined. But the statistics are, nonetheless, staggering in all the ways that fatherlessness can, and have taken a toll on her. It's because of this that teaching and transforming our men to become strong fathers that reflect the fatherhood of Father God to their children is so vitally important.

FATHERLESS SONS

Growing up without a father has a profound effect on teenage boys and young men that lasts well into their manhood. Teenage boys and young men need a father to learn how to be a man. Without having this influence in their lives, they are at risk of growing into men who have problems with their behavior, emotional stability, and close personal relationships.

Men who grew up without a father will have lower self-esteem than those who had fathers. Men learn their identity, self-worth and much of their value as a man through their relationship and interactions with a father. Teenage boys look to their fathers to encourage and affirm them, to instill that they are becoming great young men that their fathers are proud of. Without a father's approval, they can experience emotional pain, which can lead to attempts to prove themselves.

In my own life, as a result of not feeling loved and rejected by my adopted father, and my years of being fatherless, I sought my identity and approval as a young man through what the world's TV, Hollywood, and the L.A. hip scene presented as what a man should be to be loved, valued, and praised. And for me, growing up in L.A., that image was the good-looking cool guy who got all the ladies. This could be the popular guy in high school who got all the chicks, A-list actors on TV and film whom women would die for, or the rock stars and star athletes dating and hooking up with as many beautiful women as they wanted. So, having some good looks (thanks to my mother), I got into acting, immersed myself in the L.A. hip scene and nightclubs, and hooked up with as many beautiful women as I wanted, feeling this is what it meant to be a man that people admired and looked up to. I lived this lifestyle from the ages of sixteen to twenty-six, which left me empty, unloved, unfulfilled, and questioning, "What is life really about? Is this the man I really want to be?"

Men who do not receive identity, approval, and affirmation from a father will often try to prove themselves through intense competition with their peers, engaging in risky behaviors and criminal "tough guy" behavior, intended to scare the world into seeing them as men. That is why we see a large percentage of men who grow up without fathers abuse alcohol and drugs and get into trouble with law enforcement.

Men who grow up without a father also have more problems bonding with their own children. Having never experienced a father-son bond, they are unsure of how to develop that relationship with their own children. Men who had absent fathers are more likely to be absent fathers themselves.

Men who were never taught how to have healthy relationships with women by a father tend to have higher break-up and divorce rates than men who grew up with a father's influence.[10]

Manhood is often identified as a certain list of characteristics, and often, these are revealed through the kind of men they were raised by, inspired by, and even led on their faith by. Fatherhood is reflected in all the men a young boy sees. Strengthening this fatherhood, allowing the Fatherhood of God to shine through the manhood of those around him, becomes fundamental to forming a confident identity, God-loving, and Christ reflecting.

FATHERLESS MEN IN OUR CHURCHES TODAY

In the above section, "Fatherless Sons," I touched on the traits and impact of fatherlessness on men, in general, who grew up without natural fathers. In this section, I want to focus on the traits of fatherless men in our churches, from insights drawn from an article, "Traumatic Traits of Fatherless Men" *by* Joseph Mattera:

Men who experienced abandonment, neglect, or lack of affirmation from a father will struggle with insecurity and a sense of inferiority. Because of this, their personal lives and ability to minister in the church are largely impacted. The insecurity yields doubt in their own abilities, as well as doubt in others. Their sense of inferiority causes them to hide their low self-esteem, often through pride and projecting a persona full of confidence to the world. But, inside, they are full of fear.

Some men who have experienced fatherlessness have a hard time inwardly submitting to any form of spiritual authority, even if they outwardly attempt to do so. They mostly make their own decisions without getting real counsel, and if they do get counsel, they will ultimately do what they want anyway because they don't believe anyone fully looks out for their interests. They relate that counsel role as the father figure they had craved, but as they had been reliant without a father for so long, they still tend to reject that external counsel for the sake of their own.

Many fatherless men with anger and trust issues regarding fathers have a hard time when they are with those in the Body of Christ, who have been called to be spiritual fathers–especially one assigned to that (fatherless) man. They clam up and stop speaking freely, or they get nervous and try hard to know how to relate and please them, or they hide their struggles from them because they are afraid the spiritual father will use it against them and hold them back from their destiny.

Some men's insecurities result in them constantly comparing themselves with other men. If they are ministers, they compare themselves with fellow ministers in their region. They are always trying to out-do other men as if ministry were a sport. For example, I know some ministers who, when talking about themselves or their ministries, always make statements like, "Our church is growing in record numbers", or "We have the largest pastoral group in the city", or "we are the church called of God to reach the city." They use competitive language with a super-spiritual religious tinge, but it is a merely fleshly competition that is not purely motivated by the leading of the Lord.

Many fatherless men struggle to relate to their own biological and spiritual sons. Since they have not had the benefit of a natural father's input and love, many have no clue as to how they can emotionally connect with their own sons and daughters. This can then perpetuate the absent father syndrome through the generations without even meaning to.

Many fatherless men have confusion as to their purpose and identity in Christ. They have a hard time internally trying to figure out who they are and what they are called to do. They struggle with their identity. They may even be the most successful business people in the world, but they are never sure of themselves and often grapple with confusion, fear and anger, and don't understand the root cause of it all. Some of the highest suicide rates in the world are in the most affluent demographics of our nation. This shows that worldly or even ministerial success can never fill the vast void in the souls of many fatherless men.[11]

Spiritual fatherhood is a calling, and they have a role to play within our worlds. But from both the internal issues of their own fatherlessness or an external issue of trying to minister to the fatherless, these obstacles and barriers can be overcome by true spiritual fathers with the Father's heart.

THE ULTIMATE IMPACT OF FATHERLESSNESS

Children who grew up without a father or have experienced hurt, rejection, emotional wounds or major disappointments from a father will have deep wounds and residual pain from their childhood present in their adulthood. The pain and wounds from an absent father or father who was deficient, passive, performance-oriented, authoritarian, abusive, and other expressions that were not godly, often create a lens through which they, as adults, will view God.

When our fathers fail us, it's hard to have a proper view of Father God and to develop a deep, personal, loving and trusting relationship with Him. In my own life, as a result of my many years of being fatherless, I could not comprehend or relate to a loving relationship with Father God for many years after receiving Christ. I could easily relate to Jesus as my Savior, Lord, and best friend. I could relate to the Holy Spirit. He was real and manifested Himself to me and through me. I experienced His presence and power, and His gifts were flowing and operating in my life. He was another best friend in addition to Jesus. Yet, when it came to Father God, there was a disconnection and feeling that He was very distant or not there. I believed in Him and loved Him by faith, but I was not experiencing a relationship with Him as I was with my best friends, Jesus and the Holy Spirit.

After several years, as a young father to my son, James Matthew, I began to catch a picture of the love Father God has for me. My love for my son was so incredible, unconditional, and pure. Next to my wife Laura, my heart and passion to love, provide, care for, and protect him were one of my reasons for living. I would do anything for him. I would give my life for him. During those early years as a young dad knowing the Scripture, *"If you (earthly fathers) who are evil know how to give good gifts to your children,*

11

how much more will your Heavenly Father give gifts to His children who ask Him" Matthew 7:1 (ESV), I began to think about the kind of love Father God must have for me. It must be greater and far above what I could ever have as an earthly father to my son.

Another milestone moment for me, coming to know the love of Father God and having a real experiential personal relationship with Him, was through my study and meditation on the Gospel of John. I clearly saw the theme and truth throughout this Gospel of the oneness of the Father and the Son. I got a hold of the revelation that everything Jesus did was an expression of Father God in union with Him. I came to realize that in their oneness, my Heavenly Father was with me in my relationship with Christ, since day one. In each and every expression and aspect of my relationship with Christ, my Father was revealing Himself to me. From this time on, I began to see Him and know Him as my Heavenly Father—a father to the fatherless!

This is the reason why Jesus came. He came not only to save us from our sins and give us the free gift of eternal life, but to reveal God the Father and reconcile His lost children, whom He created, back to Himself. God is not a distant God, but a God who wants to love you and desires for you to know Him and be known as His precious child.

CHAPTER SUMMARY

1. Seventeen percent of children live in a single-parent household, and eighty-eight percent of these households are headed up by women.
2. The U.S. has the world's highest rate of children living in single-parent households. An estimated 24.7 million children live absent of their biological fathers.

3. The U.S. is the most prosperous nation in the world, but what is true prosperity?

4. True prosperity is the strength and multiplication of godly families that establish godly communities, cities, and nations. A nation is only as great as its fathers.

5. Fatherlessness is one of the most troubling social ills in our world. The impact on individuals and societies across the nations is truly characteristic of the curse. (Malachi 4:4-6)

6. Fatherless children are at a dramatically greater risk of drug and alcohol abuse, mental illness, suicide, poor educational performance, high school dropout, teen pregnancy, and criminality.

7. Fatherless daughters suffer from emotional trauma as a result of being fatherless. It can have a severe impact on their self-image, self-esteem, confidence, and life aspirations.

8. Fatherless young women become vulnerable to self-destructive behavior, sexual promiscuity, and often develop a pattern of unhealthy or abusive relationships with men.

9. Fatherless sons will struggle with their identity, self-esteem, insecurities, behavior, and value as a man.

10. Boys need a father to learn what it means to be a man and how to have healthy personal relationships.

11. Fatherless men in our churches often struggle with insecurities, trust issues, submitting to spiritual authority, comparison with other men, and their identity and purpose in Christ.

12. The ultimate impact of fatherlessness, or from hurts and emotional wounds from a father is seeing Father God through the lens of these experiences.

13. When our fathers fail us, it's hard to have a proper view of Father God and to develop a deep, personal, loving and trusting relationship with Him.

REFLECTION QUESTIONS

1. As you've read about the magnitude and terrible consequences of fatherlessness in our world, what can you do in your own life, family, and communities to effect change?

2. What mindsets and impact has your experience with your father or the absence of a father had upon your life?

3. How has your relationship with your father or the absence of a father affected your perspective or personal relationship with God as your Heavenly Father?

4. What are some of the steps you can take to receive healing if you have any hurts, wounds, or pain in your heart from being fatherless or from a hurtful or estranged relationship with a father?

5. What steps can you take to renew your mind to have a godly perspective of fatherhood and to see God as a loving and perfect Father?

2

"SHOW US THE FATHER"

"Show us the Father" is in the heart of every fatherless child. I have a friend, Jeff, who told me this story of when he was in junior high school, and his neighborhood buddy was loading his father's station wagon. This was back in the 1970s. He loaded the station wagon with tents, sleeping bags, luggage and ice chests, all tied to the roof, while the other five children loaded into the car. Can you imagine it? The whole family loading up for a trip together. Four days prior, Jeff and his buddy tried convincing his friend's parents to take him on the camping trip, but there just wasn't any extra room left in the car. As tears rolled down Jeff's cheeks that Saturday morning, he watched his friend and the family ride off for their vacation. His heart longed for a father and family like that one day. And that's the cry in the heart of fatherless children. They're crying out, "Show us the father."

We were created to have a relationship with our Heavenly Father, but many times, as I shared in chapter one, the image of Him is distorted by the lack of an earthly dad. A "father" is not just a noun; it's also an adjective, a descriptive action word, characterizing what a father does. My friend, Jeff, had an image that day of what a father does. And that's the kind of father that he wanted to be one day. Our world needs fathers who aren't just noun fathers, but adjective fathers, as well.

In the Gospel of John chapter 14, we read about one of Jesus's final moments and opportunities with His disciples to prepare them for their life's mission, which He would later commission them for. In this story, the disciples asked Jesus one of the most important and profound requests they had ever asked Him, a request that is relevant for all people, and for all time, "Lord, show us the Father."

> "Let not your hearts be troubled. Believe in God; believe also in Me. In My Father's house there are many rooms. If it were not so, would I have told you that I go to prepare a place for you? And if I go and prepare a place for you, I will come again and will take you to Myself, that where I am you may be also. And you know the way to where I am going." Thomas said to Him, "Lord, we do not know where You are going. How can we know the way?" Jesus said to him, "I am the Way, and the Truth, and the Life. No one comes to the Father except through Me. If you had known Me, you would have known My Father also. From now on you do know Him and have seen Him." Philip

said to Him, "Lord, show us the Father, and it is enough for us."[1] John 14:1-8 (ESV).

To provide some context to this moment, Jesus and His disciples were having a final meal together, as Jesus knew His time had come to fulfill His mission on earth. So, he had one final opportunity to teach and leave them with pillars of truth and understanding that would solidify them in their relationship with Himself and God and set the course for their future ministry as apostles and messengers of God.

Jesus begins this time with His disciples in His final lesson of love and serving one another with Him washing their feet. Then He gives them a picture of the Father's house, the place He is preparing for them, and that He would come again to take them there. He then answers their question about the way to the Father's house with a revelation in just one statement that He is the source for all of life—"I am the Way, the Truth and the Life." Afterward, He wanted them to know, beyond a shadow of a doubt, they have seen and come to know God the Father. It's amazing to me that, even though they had been with Jesus for three-and-a-half years, who did nothing outside the will of the Father, who only spoke the words of the Father, and did the works of the Father, they still didn't know if they've seen the Father. They didn't know that they knew Him or who He was. In response to Jesus giving them a picture of the Father's house in Heaven, revealing their eternal home, revealing He would come again, and that He was the way, truth, and life and only way to the Father, all that mattered in their final hours with Jesus was to know the Father that Jesus knew. Phillip said, *"Show us the Father and that is enough for us."*

There are many people around the world, even in our churches, and maybe some of you who are reading this book, who have the same questions, desires, and deep hunger in your heart and soul. You want to see and know Father God. You want to truly know God, the One you've heard about your whole life. You want to know Him, be loved by Him, and to be known by Him personally and intimately in the depth of your soul. You want to be secure as His son or daughter and know beyond a shadow of a doubt that God, as your loving Heavenly Father, will always care for you. He is always with you and will never leave you. Many of you have lots of questions regarding what He is really like. Can I really trust Him as a loving and perfect father? Am I truly His precious child that He loves greater than any earthly father could ever love their son or daughter? Are His plans perfect for me? Does He truly care for me and protects me? Is He with me every moment through every experience of my life, the good, the bad, and the ugly? Will He always provide for me? Can I truly fully believe, trust, and be at rest in His plans for me my whole life? My answer to you from the depth of my heart and soul is emphatically YES!

I will never forget, approximately six years after coming to Christ and beginning to see and know God as my Heavenly Father, I received a prophetic word for the first time where God called me His son and told me how much He loved me, and the plans He had for my life. It was at a church service with a prophetic guest minister, who called me out during the ministry time and prophesied these words to me by the Spirit of God *"Preacher man, preacher man, you waited to the end, but you, My son, will be the one I will send. I will send you to places where others will not touch; I will send you to places because I love you so much. I will trust you with newness, I will trust you with My plans, for you are My son and you are the man."* Wow! God knew me and called me His son. He truly loves and cares for me and has great and exciting plans for me. He said I was the man for the job.

18

My Heavenly Father knew my giftings to preach, teach, and evangelize, and what was in my heart. He knew my burden and passionate desire to reach the lost and to make disciples of all the nations. So, several years later, I took a step of faith and left my management job to pursue a full-time job in the ministry. Within a month, I was hired with a leading global ministry as the manager of one of their largest international ministries. It was a total God thing, as there were two candidates with great experience the executive management had narrowed it down to, but God had another plan. The managing director decided to interview one more applicant, which was me. I was brought in for an interview with him, and to his surprise, he hired me with no international ministry experience. God's favor was upon me, proving and fulfilling His prophetic promise that I would go to the nations.

Father God is a God of His Word. In this role, I led missions to reach the lost and the least of these and to equip God's ministers and people in some of the most impoverished and darkest regions of the world, places where others would not touch. God gave me tremendous favor and promoted me throughout the thirteen years I was there serving in positions as the U.S. Director of Church Relations and Director of Global Missions and Internships. Throughout my time with this international ministry, Father God provided and cared for my family and me. He protected and anointed me for my Kingdom assignments on the mission field and in churches globally. And this was just the beginning! My Heavenly Father's love, care, provision, and protection for me as I serve Him in the ministry continues to this day, approaching thirty years. He is a faithful, loving Father, and His plans are good!

"For I know the plans I have for you," declares the Lord, "plans to prosper you and not to harm you, plans to give you hope and a future" Jeremiah 29:11 (NIV).

So, this is why Jesus came to reconcile mankind back to the Father's heart and purposes for us. He came so that we may see God and truly know Him as our personal, loving Father; to know He is good and has great plans for us.

Jesus came to this earth over two thousand years ago not only to die for all of mankind's sins, to save us and reconcile us back to God, but to also reveal God as our perfect and loving Heavenly Father, who He is and what He is like. He came to reveal Father God's heart and purpose for creating us. The purpose is to have a deep, loving, and personal relationship with Him as His precious son or daughter, His eternal plan for us to be His family. A family created in His image and likeness, who would give Him great joy and pleasure!

Prior to God sending His Son, Jesus, to the earth, God's people (the Jews) we read about in the Old Testament only knew God in certain ways that were revealed and understood by them at that time. It was an incomplete picture and expression of God. In the book of Genesis, God is revealed as "Elohim", which means creator God. In chapter one, we read, *"In the beginning Elohim said 'let there be light' and there was light. Then Elohim said, 'let there be an expanse between the waters of the heavens and the earth'... then Elohim said, 'let there be lights in the sky'"* and so on... In Genesis chapter two, man comes on the scene, and God reveals Himself as Yahweh Elohim – Lord God, who is a covenant-keeping God. Then later in Genesis, God reveals Himself to Abraham at ninety-nine years old as "El Shaddai" – I am Almighty God. Abraham knew God as Creator and

Lord God, but at age ninety-nine, he came to know God as Almighty God. Then we see a progression of the Jewish revelation of God under the covenant (Old Covenant) He made with them through various names, such as Jehovah Jireh – the Lord who provides, Jehovah Rophe – the Lord who heals, Jehovah Shalom- The Lord our peace, and several others. Yet, even knowing God as Elohim, El Shaddai, Yahweh, Jehovah, and through other names, they did not know God in a deep, personal, relational and intimate way. They did not know Him as a father - someone they could know and communicate with personally just as a precious child with their daddy, and get to know His personal love and care for them. They could not approach Him because they knew He was a Holy God who had given them laws to abide by. He was distant, as they felt separated and often in fear because of their sin, always knowing they were falling short of God's laws.

There are many people today that feel the same way. You might feel as if you are always falling short of what you think God expects of you. You may not feel good enough or worthy enough to be close to God. As a result, you have never really approached Him nor knew Him in a deep, personal way as an unconditionally loving Father. Yet, you have a deep void and longing in your heart to know Him personally, to be loved and known by Him. Some of you may not even recognize it nor understand it, but you've been trying to fill this void of love through human relationships that can only be filled by the One who created you. This void and longing to be loved and known by Him is in all people because it has been created within us. We were created to be loved and known by Father God, and it is His passion and desire for you to know Him personally as His child, a member of His loving family. This is the ultimate reason why God sent His Son Jesus to the earth.

Going back to the story with Jesus and His disciples in John 14, when Phillip asked Jesus, *"Lord, show us the Father,"* Jesus answers, *"Have I been with you so long, and you still don't know Me, Phillip? Whoever has seen Me has seen the Father. How can you say 'Show us the Father'? Do you not believe that I am in the Father and the Father is in me?"* John 14:8-10 (ESV). Jesus reveals what they did not grasp and understand all along, having been with Him for three and a half years. The truth and reality that He and the Father are one.

Throughout Scripture and in the life and Words of Jesus, we see the truth of the oneness of Jesus and the Father, and that in everything Christ did was not only an expression of Himself, but an expression from God the Father:

"I and the Father are one" John 10:30 (ESV).

"He is the visible image of the invisible God…For in Him all the fullness of God was pleased to dwell" Colossians 1:15, 19 (ESV).

"For I have come down from Heaven not to do My will but to do the will of Him who sent Me" John 6:38 (ESV).

"I do not ask for these only, but also for those who will believe in Me through their word, that they may all be one, just as you, Father, are in Me, and I am in You" John 17:20-21 (ESV).

"I say to you the Son can do nothing of His own accord, but only what He sees the Father doing. Whatever the Father does, that the Son does likewise" John 5:19 (ESV).

If you want to know what the Father is like, who He is, His character, nature, and the love that He has for us, look no further and look at the life and person of Jesus. He is the One who came to introduce us, show us, and reconcile us to the Father. Jesus said, *"I am the way... No one comes to the Father except through Me"* John 14:6 (ESV).

Let's also look at a few of my favorite stories from the life and teachings of Jesus that powerfully show us God's desire for us to know Him as Father, and His incredible heart, nature, and love for us as an unconditional loving Father:

THE WOMAN AT THE WELL

"So He left Judea and returned to Galilee. He had to go through Samaria on the way. Eventually He came to the Samaritan village of Sychar, near the field that Jacob gave to his son Joseph. Jacob's well was there; and Jesus, tired from the long walk, sat wearily beside the well about noontime. Soon a Samaritan woman came to draw water, and Jesus said to her, "Please give me a drink." He was alone at the time because His disciples had gone into the village to buy some food. The woman was surprised, for Jews refuse to have anything to do with Samaritans. She said to Jesus, "You are a Jew, and I am a Samaritan woman. Why are You asking me for a drink?" Jesus replied, "If you only knew the gift God has for you and who you are speaking to, you would ask Me, and I would give you living water." "But sir, You don't have a rope or a bucket," she said, "and this well is very deep. Where would You get this living water? And besides, do You think You're greater than our ancestor Jacob, who gave us

this well? How can you offer better water than he and his sons and his animals enjoyed?" Jesus replied, "Anyone who drinks this water will soon become thirsty again. But those who drink the water I give will never be thirsty again. It becomes a fresh, bubbling spring within them, giving them eternal life." "Please, Sir," the woman said, "give me this water! Then I'll never be thirsty again, and I won't have to come here to get water." "Go and get your husband," Jesus told her. "I don't have a husband," the woman replied. Jesus said, "You're right! You don't have a husband— for you have had five husbands, and you aren't even married to the man you're living with now. You certainly spoke the truth!" "Sir," the woman said, "You must be a prophet. So tell me, why is it that you Jews insist that Jerusalem is the only place of worship, while we Samaritans claim it is here at Mount Gerizim, where our ancestors worshiped?" Jesus replied, "Believe Me, dear woman, the time is coming when it will no longer matter whether you worship the Father on this mountain or in Jerusalem. You Samaritans know very little about the One you worship, while we Jews know all about Him, for salvation comes through the Jews. But the time is coming—indeed it's here now—when true worshipers will worship the Father in spirit and in truth. The Father is looking for those who will worship Him that way. For God is Spirit, so those who worship Him must worship in spirit and in truth." The woman said, "I know the Messiah is coming—the one who is called Christ. When He comes, He will explain everything to us." Then Jesus told her, "I am the Messiah!"² John 4:3-26 (ESV).

Here, we see a couple of powerful truths about the Father's heart and love through Christ. The Samaritans were a mixed raced people, who had intermarried with the Assyrians, centuries before, so they were hated and rejected by the Jews. Also, she was a woman who was known and shamed by her community because of her multiple marriages and sexual immorality living with a man whom she was not married to. As a Jew and rabbi, it would have never been imaginable for Jesus to ever approach this Samaritan woman. We see later in the story, the shock of the disciples that Jesus was even speaking with her. They did not know nor understand Father God's heart and the love and compassion He has for all people.

Jesus saw a broken woman who had been starving for the love of a man her whole life, entering into one marriage after another, never ever feeling loved, accepted, and always rejected. Maybe she never was fully loved by an earthly father. So, as a result, she tried to fill the void of the absence of the love of a father and went from one man to another. Men married her and used her for however long, then divorced her when she no longer served their purposes. I don't know the depth of what was going on in her heart, but I do know the story reveals there were tremendous brokenness and a void for a love that only Father God could heal and fill. A void that she was also trying to fill through religious duties. Recognizing Jesus was a prophet, she asked Jesus the question of where one should worship.

Notice, it's clear she had been participating in the religion of her culture by asking this question. It's also evident that her religion had not filled the void for love and spiritual life she was so desperately hungering and thirsting for. Jesus, knowing her brokenness and desperate need, points her to the only One who could fill this void and thirst and love her unconditionally. The only One who could heal her heart and soul and give her a new life. He introduces her to the One "The Father" who desires true worshippers who will worship Him in Spirit and truth. He shows her the way to a relationship with the Father through Himself. A life of spending time with the Father in His loving presence through worship that comes from receiving Jesus, who is the truth and by the Holy Spirit, who leads us into His presence. Jesus being one with the Father, manifests a "Father-daughter" moment, a loving Father who longs to forgive, heal, love, and restore a daughter who was lost back to Himself.

My wife, Laura, grew up without a father, being raised by a single mother with two older sisters. She had no father figure in her life throughout her childhood, adolescence, and into her adulthood. It had a great impact on her life and behavior as a child and young adult. She remembers the many times that she saw friends who were close to their fathers ("daddy's girls") and how it made her feel sad that she did not have a relationship with her father. Her parents were divorced, leaving my wife and her sisters without a father when they were very young. When she started dating, she had no guide, good or bad, so she made some poor choices in her relationships with men. She was extremely insecure and found herself relying on others to make her feel secure. She hung out with the wrong crowd and found herself lost after a while.

At the age of twenty-six, she made a new friend, who was a Christian. Her friend invited her to church, and in attending the worship service, she received Christ as her savior. She fell in love with God's presence and could not get enough of spending time with God. After six months into her walk with God, she left her boyfriend because she recognized it was an ungodly relationship. She was alone, and for the first time in her life, she found joy and comfort in not needing a man for happiness. She continued to spend time with God going to church and doing daily devotions, and through this time, she came to know Father God in a deep, personal way. He was loving, caring, calming, and was always with her. He healed her from her life of emptiness and hurt. She was secure and at peace with being alone; no one to come home to except to Him. She met the One, the only One who could truly fill the void in her heart and love her unconditionally just as she is, God her Father.

With the story of the Woman at the Well, we see the truth of an unconditionally loving Father, who loves all people of every race, ethnicity, gender, and culture, regardless of how abhorrent or sinful your life may be in the eyes of man and religion. He's a Father who will go out of His way to reach out and introduce Himself to you and welcome you into a relationship with Him as a loving daughter or son. This is a perfect love relationship that can never be found in a human relationship, or through religion or religious duties, but only through a personal relationship with Him through His Son, Jesus Christ.

THE LOST SON

"Jesus told them this story: 'A man had two sons. The younger son told his father, 'I want my share of your estate now before you die.' So his father agreed to divide his wealth between his sons. "A few days later this younger son packed all his belongings and moved to a distant land, and there he wasted all his money in wild living. About the time his money ran out, a great famine swept over the land, and he began to starve. He persuaded a local farmer to hire him, and the man sent him into his fields to feed the pigs. The young man became so hungry that even the pods he was feeding the pigs looked good to him. But no one gave him anything. "When he finally came to his senses, he said

to himself, 'At home even the hired servants have food enough to spare, and here I am dying of hunger! I will go home to my father and say, "Father, I have sinned against both Heaven and you, and I am no longer worthy of being called your son. Please take me on as a hired servant." "So he returned home to his father. And while he was still a long way off, his father saw him coming. Filled with love and compassion, he ran to his son, embraced him, and kissed him. His son said to him, 'Father, I have sinned against both heaven and you, and I am no longer worthy of being called your son.' "But his father said to the servants, 'Quick! Bring the finest robe in the house and put it on him. Get a ring for his finger and sandals for his feet. And kill the calf we have been fattening. We must celebrate with a feast, for this son of mine was dead and has now returned to life. He was lost, but now he is found.' So the party began"[3]
Luke 15:11-24 (NLT).

In this parable, we see a powerful truth and expression of Father God's nature, heart, and unconditional love toward a lost son or daughter. In the culture of the day, a son's inheritance was not to come to him until after the passing of his father. By asking for his inheritance early, the younger son was essentially saying I wish you were dead so I can have my inheritance. It would have been one of the most serious acts of dishonor a son could give to his father, that according to the Jewish law, could have warranted a punishment of being stoned. But the father was different, he was full of love and mercy, and without anger or judgment, and despite his son's rebellion, he gave him his inheritance.[4] And when the rebellious son left and squandered his inheritance on reckless and immoral living, the father looked out for him daily to come back home. After the son has nothing left and hits rock bottom, he comes to his senses with a desire to return to his father, hoping to be received no longer as a son but as a servant. The father sees him far off and runs to embrace him with his unfailing love and compassion, restoring him as his son and celebrating his return to His house.

Jesus reveals to us through this parable of the incredible unconditional love and compassion the Father has for those who are lost or have left Him. His love, grace, and mercy are never-ending and unfailing toward us. Even when you rebel or walk away from a relationship with Him, and live in ways that are ungodly and destructive, the Father is always looking out for you and waiting for you to come back home. He will never give up on you. He is always there for you and will never leave you nor fail you. He will forgive and restore you to the fullness for which you have been created - a royal son or daughter, an ambassador of His royal family and kingdom.

I have a spiritual son named Dan who gave his life to the Lord as a teenager, but as a young adult, he walked away and started partying heavily, with drinking and smoking pot as part of his lifestyle as a drummer in a rock band. In his early twenties, he got married to his wife, Kelly, who also did drugs and did not know Christ. Within a few years, they had two children, a girl named Brittany and a boy named Brandon. When Brittany was two and Brandon was just a baby, Dan left his wife, Kelly, to pursue another woman who was a huge fan of the rock band he was a member of.

He continued his partying ways, spending time with this woman, and was on the verge of entering into a physical adulterous relationship. But Father God never stopped loving and looking out for Dan. Hence, through his praying mom (who prayed for him daily), He invited him and his estranged wife, Kelly, of six months to a prophetic ministry meeting where I was ministering. His mom also invited his brother, who was a non-believer, to this ministry meeting, as she was a regular attendee to my meetings. During the ministry time of my meeting, I began to pray and prophesy over Dan's brother, speaking on things about his life and who he was as an athlete. Dan was blown away by this, as I've never met him nor knew anything about him and his life. After I prayed for his brother, Dan came up with Kelly to receive prayer. As I prayed for him and Kelly and gently laid my hands on them, they fell out under the presence and power of God, where they laid on the floor for about fifteen minutes.

God did supernatural surgery on their hearts. After getting up from this supernatural encounter and touch from God, Dan rededicated his life to Christ, with Kelly also giving her life to Christ. God did a miracle of reconciliation that night, reconciling Dan back to Himself as His son, and him back to his wife and children, his true inheritance. Today, seventeen years later, they have seven kids and have been loving and serving God faithfully since that night. Father God's love never gave up on Dan, restoring him as His royal son, and the godly father he was created and destined to be.

ABBA FATHER

Jesus' life showed us and gave us the greatest name that encompasses all other names of who God is to us, and that name is "Father." In John's Gospel, Jesus calls God His Father 156 times and, on several occasions, uses the term "Abba Father." Abba, the Aramaic word for "Daddy," is a very comfortable and intimate term that describes a deep, personal relationship a child has with their father as "Daddy." The childlike faith and trust he or she puts in daddy's love and care. Jesus calling God his personal Father or Abba was blasphemous to the Jews, but Jesus reveals the true nature and heart of God toward us as a loving personal Father and Daddy. Not only did Jesus call God "Abba," He taught us to know Him as our Father and to call Him Abba. He taught us that there is a Heavenly Father who knows all our needs and will provide them before we even utter one word. So, when we pray, we should say, "Our *Abba Father* in Heaven, Holy be your name..." Luke 11:2.

When we come to know God as Abba Father, His perfect love will cast out all fear, and we will forever know and trust we are loved, accepted, and cared for. *"So you have not received a spirit that makes you fearful slaves. Instead, you received God's Spirit when He adopted you as His own children. Now we call Him, "Abba, Father"* Romans 8:15 (NLT).

CHAPTER SUMMARY

1. Jesus is the way, the truth, and the life. He is the only way to Father God. Knowing the Father is the true destiny of our faith. John 14:6

2. Jesus came to reveal the Father so that we may see and truly come to know Him as a perfect, loving, and faithful Father.

3. Prior to Jesus' coming to the earth, the people of God had an incomplete picture, experience, and understanding of God. They did not know Him as their personal Father.

4. Many people around the world, and even in our churches, have an incomplete picture, understanding, and relationship with God as a perfect loving Father, but in their hearts, they long to see and know Him as a perfect loving Father.

5. There will always be a deep longing and void in your heart for a perfect love that no human relationship can fulfill. Only God, the Father, can fill this void because we were created to be known and loved by Him.

6. Religion cannot heal brokenness and fill the void for love and true spiritual life that only a relationship with Father God, through Jesus Christ, can heal and fulfill.

7. Father God is always looking out for you, and He's waiting for you to come to Him or come back to Him if you run away.

8. No sin or destructive behavior will ever keep you from the Father's unfailing love and compassion, who longs to restore you as His royal son or daughter.

9. Father God wants you to know Him as "Abba Father". A deep, personal, intimate, and trusting relationship just as a child on earth has with their father as 'Daddy".

10. The Father's perfect love casts out all fear, causing us to know and trust we are always loved, cared for, and protected by Him.

REFLECTION QUESTIONS

1. In the depth of your heart, do you know God in a deep personal way as your loving and perfect Heavenly Father? If not, what do you think are the reasons? If yes, how has He revealed Himself to you?

2. What doubts, struggles or mindsets have kept you from knowing and having a deep personal relationship with God as your Father?

3. Do you have a deep personal relationship with Jesus? How has Jesus, being one with the Father, revealed and shown the Father to you?

4. What does it mean to you to know Father God as "Abba" or "Daddy"?

5. Did you know in your heart there is no sin or destructive behavior that the Father cannot forgive and set you free from, nor keep Him from loving you? If not, what are the mindsets keeping you from receiving His forgiveness and love?

6. Ask God to forgive, cleanse, and heal you from anything that is keeping you from turning to Him. Write down the areas that you want God to remove and wipe away from your life.

7. Receive God's restoration to your true identity as His royal son or daughter. Ask Him what it means to be His child - a loving royal son or daughter.

3

THE FATHERHOOD OF GOD

THE FATHERHOOD OF GOD
THROUGH GODLY FATHERS

"Then God said, "Let Us make man in Our image, after our
likeness… So God created man in His own image, in the image
of God He created him; male and female He created them.
And God blessed them. And God said to them, "Be fruitful
and multiply and fill the earth…" Genesis 1:26-28 (ESV).

In the very beginning, we see that man was created to be a visible image and representation of God on earth, who he is (image) and what he is like (likeness). And in this, He created male and female differently to fulfill unique roles and to reveal and reflect different facets of Himself in their marriage-union and family. The man, a picture and reflection of God Himself, as a husband to his bride, and as a father to his children. To confirm this foundational truth, we read in Ephesians chapter five that husbands are to love their wives as Christ loves the Church; and as fathers, they are to teach and train up their children in the instruction of the Lord.

As the Father in Christ loves and teaches us, so should our Heavenly Father be revealed and seen in husbands and fathers, as they love their wives, care for, and teach their children. God has not only revealed Himself as a loving Father through the life and person of Christ, He's also created and purposed men to become fathers and to reveal Himself to their children as a loving father through their fatherhood. God's design for children is to learn about the fatherhood of God through the role of a godly father in the family.

I shared in chapter one that the ultimate impact of fatherlessness is the fatherless seeing God through the lens of their experience, or lack of experience, with a father that prevents them from having a relationship with, knowing, or trusting God as a loving Heavenly Father. Fathers speak about God the Father constantly, whether it is a true representation or false one. This is a critical truth to understand in God's design and purpose for godly fathers. As we unconditionally love, provide, care for, and protect our children, they will learn to see and know God's love and care for them as their Heavenly Father.

I shared a glimpse of my testimony as a young father, how I came to see and know my Heavenly Father through my fatherhood with my son, James Matthew. In the same way, children will come to see and know Father God's love for them through the love, care, and protection from their natural fathers. My youngest son, Ethan, who is eighteen years old, has never had any serious concerns, worries, or fear about his life. He's always felt loved, cared for, and secure in his childhood and teen years because he knows he has a father who loves him and will always provide and protect him. He knows he belongs to his father's house, and all that I have, he has access to. He knows his father's desire is to bless him and help him succeed in all that he does. In this season of his life, he's ready to launch out to go to college, work, and begin living life as a more independent young adult. He's confident in moving forward because just as his dad has always been there for him, he knows Father God will provide and take care of him. He's secure in his identity as a son in whom God loves, a Father in Heaven, whom he can believe and trust in.

The apostle, Paul, reveals to us in his letter to the Ephesians that all fatherhood on earth is connected to and derives its name from God the Father. *"For this reason grasping the greatness of this plan by which Jews and Gentiles are joined together in Christ, I bow my knees in reverence before the Father of our Lord Jesus Christ, from whom every family in Heaven and on earth derives its name God—the first and ultimate Father"* Ephesians 3:14-15 (AMP). This means that a human father is named and claimed in the image of the eternal Father. He is called to be a godly father on earth like the Father is in Heaven so that his children can hear, see, and touch the Father in Heaven through him. He is the voice of the Father that his child cannot hear, the face of the Father that his child cannot see, the touch of the Father his child cannot feel. A godly father is the visible icon of the Heavenly Father.[1]

Some of you men reading this right now may be asking yourself, how can I be a reflection of Father God to my children when I've had no father or model of a godly father in my life? The good news for the fatherless is God is the ultimate restorer and teacher. He can restore what we've lost or give us what we never had and use it to teach us His fatherhood, as we come to know and experience Him through a relationship with Christ. He is a father to the fatherless. In Christ, the fatherless are no longer fatherless. This has been my journey and experience for the last twenty-nine years since giving my life to Christ and being in a relationship with Him and my Heavenly Father. It's an ongoing learning and growing process in becoming more like Christ, and a father like Father God is to us. You will not always get it right, you will make lots of mistakes as a father to your children, but you will do a lot of things right and experience great blessing and joy when you see your children grow and thrive throughout their childhood and adolescence.

For those of you that feel it's too late to be the godly father you wished you could have been because your children are grown adults now, they have been out of the house for years, for some, a decade or two, let me share with you about my dear friend, Tony, who is also a spiritual father to me. Tony is a successful attorney who was a big shot for many years running his law firm in multiple cities, but he admits that throughout this season of his life he was not a very good father to his son and was absent in many ways. Because of his deficiencies as a father, and his mistakes, this caused a serious strain and distance in his relationship with his son, which lasted for many years. Tony was a believer in Christ through these years, having given his life to Christ when he was young, but he did not really live for Him until far later in his life. He didn't really know what it meant to be a fully devoted follower of Christ and to be established in His identity as a son of Father God. Tony admits and often testifies that it took him decades, not until he was age sixty, to discover his identity as a true son of Father God. Not until this time did he realize what it meant to live as a follower of Christ and live as a godly husband to his wife, and godly father to his grown children.

Today, Tony is in his late seventies, and for the past eighteen years, he has been the godly father he's always wanted to be to his son and daughters. This has brought great restoration to his relationship with his son and blessing to his stepdaughters, whom God brought into his life. Tony often tells me his transformation came after forty years of him receiving Christ, by the renewing of his mind through the Word of God, and through spending time daily with his Heavenly Father.

Fathers, it's never too late to be a reflection of the fatherhood of God and the godly father you were created to be. The apostle, Paul, reveals a powerful truth that applies to every father who has given his life to Father God - *"Being confident of this, that He who began a good work in you will carry it on to completion until the day of Christ Jesus"* Philippians 1:6 (NIV).

THE FATHERHOOD OF GOD
THROUGH SPIRITUAL FATHERS

Fatherhood is not merely or essentially biological. Any man can be a biological father, but it takes a real man to be a godly and spiritual father. A godly father understands his responsibility and role is not only to care, provide, and protect his children, but he is to be a spiritual father, one who teaches his children in the instruction of the Lord and ways of God. Spiritual fatherhood is the vehicle for the fatherhood of God to learn His Word, ways, wisdom, and instruction to live by His Spirit. Ephesians 6:4 tells us, *"Fathers, do not provoke your children to anger, but bring them up in the discipline and instruction of the Lord."* Notice how this responsibility is given to the fathers. This is seen not only in the book of Ephesians, but this charge was given to fathers as a commandment in the Old Testament. *"Hear, O Israel: The Lord our God, the Lord is one. Love the Lord your God with all your heart and with all your soul and with all your strength. These commandments that I give you today are to be on your hearts. Impress them on your children. Talk about them when you sit at home and when you walk along the road, when you lie down and when you get up"[2]* Deuteronomy 6:4-6 (NIV). So, we see both in the Old and New Testament that fathers are essential in not only reflecting the Father, but in teaching and imparting the ways of Father God to their children.

As a full-time pastor, my son, Ethan, attended church with me on Sundays throughout his childhood and teens, so he received a lot of Bible teaching, instruction, and spiritual guidance at church through the children's ministry and midweek youth ministry meetings. As a result, I did not add more personal Bible studies throughout his week or insist on daily or weekly devotions with dad. However, I understood as a godly father it was my responsibility to be his spiritual father, to model living for God, pray for him daily, and to teach him the Word and ways of God. This responsibility was not given to the children or youth ministry leaders.

So, instead of having a personal Bible study or devotions with him, I would have conversations throughout the week about what he was learning in the youth ministry meetings. We would talk about his life, what he was experiencing in school, his friends, and things he was involved in. We would also talk about what was going on in our world, culture, current events and things we would see and experience when spending time together having a meal, having coffee, riding bikes, bowling, or catching a movie. In all our times and discussions together, I found opportunities for teaching and mentoring moments, and times that I could pray with him. As I was led by the Holy Spirit, I would share biblical truth, instruction, or guidance in a very organic, conversational, and relational way. I did not have to quote the Scriptures but spoke and taught him the truth of God's Word and instruction for living in the language that he could understand and receive.

I found this effective and has borne great fruit, as Ethan has grown to become an incredible young man who loves and knows Father God, and continues to grow in knowing and living out His truth and ways. He's not perfect and has made mistakes along the way, but his heart is for God and standing for truth. He's a loving, compassionate, and generous soul, who loves helping and serving others.

What I shared is an example of an approach to spiritual fatherhood that I believe is what Deuteronomy 6:4-6 is describing—spiritual fatherhood throughout daily living in relationship with our children.

Another example I want to share with you comes from a friend of mine, Jael, whose father, Jim, has been a great example of spiritual fatherhood to his children. Jael shares, "My dad is a man of prayer. Throughout my entire childhood, I remember seeing him in the early hours of the morning in his prayer chair with his Bible in hand, praying. There was never a morning that went by that he was not praying for our family, our country, our church and anything and anyone else the Lord put on his heart to intercede for. As a child, I didn't fully understand why my dad would wake up at 3:40am to be ready to start praying by 4am, so he could have one full hour with the Lord before leaving for work. Even on the weekends and holidays, he would still get up early; not quite as early, but still with the same passion for the Word and prayer.

He did something that seemed 'funny' to me that I later asked him about. 'Why do you move your hand up and down and then around in a circle while you pray?' I asked with a touch of laughter in my voice. My dad responded, 'I am pleading the blood of Jesus on you, your brother and your mom from the tops of your heads to the soles of your feet. And I am praying a hedge of fire protection around each of you.' I will always remember that answer. It was at that moment that I really knew my dad was covering me in prayer every day. My dad's faithfulness and consistency have taught me to be faithful and consistent with my time with the Lord, too. He has modeled for me to start my day with the Lord, reading His Word and praying the Word. And now, in retirement, my dad still gets up early to meet with the Lord.

My relationship with my dad has taught me so much about Father God. Father God is constant and faithful. He has my back before I even know I need the protection. He is constantly fighting for me and is my safe refuge. He ultimately wants me to succeed, but will lead and help guide me along the way. At the end of the day, His love for me outweighs everything. I know my dad loves me wholeheartedly, so I can't even fathom how much Father God loves me."

The fatherhood of God through spiritual fatherhood is not only for godly fathers to be spiritual fathers with their natural children, but applies to spiritual fathers to father and raise up even non-biological spiritual children. In Malachi 4:6, we read, *"And He will turn the hearts of the fathers to the children, and the hearts of the children to their fathers."* The term fathers and children were not just referring to fathers and their biological children, but a call for spiritual fathers to turn to and raise up spiritual children. We also see this truth of spiritual fathers and spiritual children in the churches in the book of 1ˢᵗ John. There are three classifications of individuals that the apostle John describes in the Churches to whom he is writing to. *"I am writing to you, dear children, because your sins have been forgiven on account of His name. I am writing to you, fathers, because you know Him who is from the beginning. I am writing to you, young men, because you have overcome the evil one. I write to you, dear children, because you know the Father. I write to you, fathers, because you know Him who is from the beginning. I write to you, young men, because you are strong, and the Word of God lives in you, and you have overcome the evil one*"[3] 1 John 2:12-14 (NIV). Notice the apostle, John, writes to the children—"you know the Father." This reveals a powerful truth of the relationships they had had in the church that resulted in them knowing the Father. They had come to know Father God because they had relationships with spiritual fathers among them who loved them and taught them the Word of God in order for them to overcome sin and the evil one. These spiritual fathers raised them to become strong, young sons and daughters.

We also see the truth of spiritual fatherhood through the life of the apostle, Paul, identifying Timothy and Titus as his spiritual sons: *"Timothy, my dear son, be strong through the grace that God gives you in Christ Jesus. You have heard me teach things that have been confirmed by many reliable witnesses. Now teach these truths to other trustworthy people who will be able to pass them on to others"* 2 Timothy 2:1 (NLT). And later in Titus, he says, *"I am writing to Titus, my true son in the faith that we share"* Titus 1:4 (NLT).

Over the years as a pastor and leader of global ministries, I've had the privilege to serve as a spiritual father to many young adults, adults, and emerging ministry leaders for seasons of their life. Some of these relationships have been for short seasons and others for longer. One example is in my previous roles as a director of global missions and internships. I served as a spiritual father-leader, teaching and mentoring over six hundred young adults as interns and missionaries through training academies, church ministries, outreaches, and global missions that I led. I taught them the Word of God, leadership, and practical ministry skills. During that time, many of them shared with me that what had had the deepest impact on their lives was how I modeled Christ and Father God through loving and serving others and how I had modeled godly leadership.

The other key that had been impactful on their lives was my being present with them with the heart of Father God in an authentic, loving, and caring relationship with them. I had taken the time to talk with them individually about their lives, their life's calling, their dreams, aspirations, struggles, and their challenges. Through these times, I was able to provide vision, direction, guidance, affirmation, and encouragement of Father God's love and purpose for them. This strengthened them to believe in themselves, pursue their dreams, step out in faith, and take the necessary steps to move forward after their internship. Spiritual fatherhood, even for a short season, made a big difference in this stage of their lives. There was a cry and a hunger for someone to believe in them and show them the way, and through spiritual fatherhood, they had experienced life-changing times, knowing they have a Heavenly Father that loves and believes in them! It is one of my most treasured honors to have been this spiritual father to them, one that I will never forget.

THE FATHERHOOD OF GOD THROUGH MODERN APOSTOLIC FATHERS

To begin, there are many churches and believers who do not believe, nor understand that the role and ministry of apostles are for us today. So, here are three key passages of Scripture that provide us a basis for the gift, function, and ministry of the apostles (apostolic fathers) today. I'll begin with: *"Together, we are His house, built on the foundation of the apostles and the prophets. And the cornerstone is Christ Jesus Himself"* Ephesians 2:20 (NLT). In this passage, we see that Jesus did not only founded the Church, but He also built into it a dynamic for ongoing expansion and development. He gave us the revelation that He wanted His followers to see Him as the cornerstone of the Church, which He would be building through the centuries, and that His design for the foundation was the apostles and prophets.[4] As Christ continues to build His Church around the world, as He has been doing for two thousand years, He is still using men and women, whom He calls and commissions, as His apostles.

Another foundational passages of Scripture for the role and ministry of apostle is found in Ephesians chapter 4: *"And he gave the apostles, the prophets, the evangelists, the shepherds and teachers, to equip the saints for the work of ministry, for building up the body of Christ, until we all attain to the unity of the faith and of the knowledge of the Son of God, to mature manhood, to the measure of the stature of the fullness of Christ"* Ephesians 4:11-12 (ESV). In these Bible passages, we see that Christ Himself created apostles for several key functions: to build His Church and to equip His people (sons and daughters) for the work of ministry. In verse 13, we see what the end game is: their role in ministry, which is Christ's global Church obtaining unity of the faith in our knowledge of Christ and His Kingdom, and His people reaching full maturity with the full stature of Christ Himself.

It's clear that Christ's Church and followers have not fulfilled that purpose; therefore, Christ's apostles are still needed and should be functioning today. This is God's design and order for His Church until we become all He has destined for us, and all the nations of the world have become discipled and transformed (Matthew 28:19). Christ's Church and His people will not become all that God has destined for us, nor will His Kingdom expand across every sphere of society without the office and ministry of apostles.

The final passage that supports their office and ministry today is found in 1 Corinthians chapter 12: *"And God has appointed in the Church first apostles, second prophets, third teachers, then miracles, then gifts of healing, helping, administrating, and various kinds of tongues"* 1 Corinthains12:28 (ESV). This passage reveals two key truths. First, the office and ministry of the apostle is a role and ministry that should be functioning in the Church today. Second, the apostles are first as it relates to the leadership structure and spiritual authority of the Church. The word 'first' in the original language is *proton*, which means first in place, rank, and order of importance.

There are many characteristics, facets, and functions of the ministry of the apostle that we see throughout the new testament, but the main role and key function that God has purposed, which is seen in a true apostle is to be, and function as an apostolic father with the heart of Father God. They are to provide spiritual fatherhood to spiritual sons and daughters, churches, and communities whom God entrusts to them. Apostolic fathers are the vehicle in which God's fatherhood is seen, flows to, and functions through Christ's Church to redeem and restore all things on the earth to the image and purposes of Christ. The apostle, Paul, encapsulates this call and heart of an apostolic father to those whom God entrusts in these verses: *"For though you have countless guides in Christ, you do not have many fathers. For I became your father in Christ Jesus through the Gospel"* 1 Corinthians 4:15 (ESV). *"My children, with whom I am again in labor until Christ is formed in you"* Galatians 4:19 (NASB).

CHAPTER SUMMARY

1. God made man in His image and likeness to reflect and reveal Him on earth and to fulfill specific roles to reflect different facets of Himself (Genesis 1:26-28).

2. The man is to be a picture and reflection of Father God to his wife as a husband and father to His children.

3. As the Father's love is expressed through Christ to us as God's children, so also is the Father's love to be expressed through earthly fathers to their children.

4. The ultimate impact of fatherlessness or deficient or hurtful fatherhood is seeing God the Father through the lens of past experiences.

5. Fathers are to always speak to their children about Father God, whether it is a true reflection or not.

6. As fathers unconditionally love, provide, care for, and protect their children, they will learn about and be able to see the love and care their Heavenly Father has for them.

7. A father is called to be a godly father on earth like the Father is in Heaven.

8. A godly father understands his role is not only to care, provide, and protect his children, but to be a spiritual father who teaches his children in the instruction of the Lord.

9. Spiritual fatherhood is the vehicle for us to learn the Fatherhood of God, His Word, truth, wisdom, and instructions for living by His spirit.

10. The fatherhood of God, through spiritual fathers, is not just to their biological children but the call and heart to father and raise up spiritual children. (Malachi 4:6)

11. God has given apostles to build His Church, equip the saints for the work of the ministry, establish unity, and grow God's people to full maturity as Christ.

12. There are many facets and ministries of an apostle, but one of the main roles and functions of a true apostle is to be an apostolic father

to spiritual sons and daughters, church families, and communities God entrusts to them.

REFLECTION QUESTIONS

1. What does it mean to you that fathers on earth are called to be godly fathers on earth as Father God is in Heaven?

2. What expression, behavior, and actions, as a father, do you feel reflects Father God well?

3. What behavior or actions, as a father, do you recognize that does not reflect Father God well or does so falsely, that needs to be adjusted, changed, or eliminated from your fathering?

4. In addition to providing, caring for, and protecting your biological children, how are you providing spiritual fatherhood in their life? How can you develop and strengthen this responsibility of your godly fatherhood?

5. Are there children in your extended family, neighborhood, and circles of life that are in need of spiritual fatherhood that you can be a spiritual father to? What steps can you take to make a difference?

6. Is God calling you to be a spiritual father in your church family? How can you serve in this capacity, and who is God calling you to reach out to?

7. If you are a pastor or spiritual father of a church or ministry, is God calling you to a higher level as an apostolic father? If so, what does that look like to you? What steps can you take to start functioning as an apostolic father?

4

BECOMING A SON OF GOD TO BECOME A GODLY FATHER

For in Christ Jesus you are all sons of God, through faith
Galatians 3:26 (ESV).

We've learned that fathers on earth are called to be vessels and re-flections of the fatherhood of God to their children, connecting them to the knowledge and relationship with Father God in Heaven. If men have not had a model of a godly father in their homes or were without a father, it is not only a great hindrance to knowing and having a deep personal relationship with God as Father; it is a major barrier to knowing how to *be* a godly father. Men who have not had godly fathers will not know what godly fatherhood looks like, due to the absence of a father, or have a distorted view from growing up with an ungodly, neglectful, or hurtful father. They would not have been taught or learned what it means, nor had the opportunity to grow into a godly father with the ongoing guidance and wisdom from a godly father. As a result, they often become like their earthly fathers, having been taught by their experiences with them.

If they have not had a father, they will become what is modeled by their peers and culture, or whatever they feel fathers should be, based on their own thinking and capacity to be a father. For some, the cycle of dysfunctional, ungodly, or absentee fatherhood continues, but for others, they desire to become the father they never had. They know in their hearts there is a better way, and that fatherhood is a true calling, and one of life's greatest purposes and blessings to have and raise up godly and successful children. This desire and purpose are created within them by their creator, Father God. It is the longing of every man's heart who has been created in the image of God.

Now, one may have a desire and choose to become a godly father, but it does not happen by desire and choice alone. Men must be taught and shown how to function and live as one and understand it is an ongoing learning and fluid journey. And the good news is, regardless of our upbringing, past, and current experiences, we can learn and become the fathers that God has created us to be. Jesus has made and shown us the way—the way to the Father to become like Him. Jesus said, *"I am the way and the truth and the life. No one comes to the Father except through Me"* (John 14:6).

The only way we can become a godly father like Father God is to first become a son by receiving Jesus Christ, who came to reveal and reconcile us back to the Father. We must give our whole lives to God as our Father so that we can learn and experience what true godly fatherhood is like. We must experience who He is, His nature, character, and ways by spending time with Him in His presence daily in order to then be transformed into His image, to reflect Him. The apostle, Paul, describes this truth and dynamic in his letter to the Corinthian Church: *"So all of us who have had that veil removed can see and reflect the glory of the Lord. And the Lord—who is the Spirit—makes us more and more like Him as we are changed into His glorious image"* 2 Corinthians 3:18 (NLT).

The veil is removed when we give our lives to God through Christ and become His sons, positioning us to see the Father as He is so that we can know Him and live like Him. If we can't see Him and know Him as He truly is, we will not be able to reflect and live like Him as a true son and godly father. As sons, we must have a daily relationship with our Heavenly Father, through Christ and by His Spirit, to experience and know His love, nature, and heart. Through this relationship, we are taught His truth, wisdom, and ways, and learn to hear and follow His voice and how to be led by His Spirit. We receive training in His righteousness and godliness, which will also include correction and discipline, when needed, as His loving son. Being taught, trained, corrected, and disciplined by the Father is proof of His love for you and evidence of being received as a son. God's Word reveals this powerful truth:

> *"For whom the Lord loves He corrects, Just as a father the son in whom he delights"* Proverbs 3:12 (NKJV).

> *"My son, think of the Lord's training as important. Do not lose hope when He corrects you. The Lord trains the one He loves. He corrects everyone He accepts as His son"* Hebrews 12: 5-6 (NIRV).

As a son, we are to continually grow and mature into a deeper and intimate relationship with Him each day, where we experience continual transformation into His image as a son like Christ, and as a father like Him. A relationship where we are so close to Him, we become more and more like Him, we become joined and one with who He is. One where His nature as Father becomes our nature as a father, His heart as Father becomes our heart, His mind as Father becomes our mind, His will as Father becomes our will, His life as Father becomes our life as a father. This is God's design and purpose for fathers, and the good news is we are not alone in this great calling and responsibility. The wonderful truth is Jesus not only showed us the Father, but He also modeled His life as God's Son, and promises, with the Holy Spirit, to be alongside us in our life as a son as we learn, grow, and live, revealing the Father through our fatherhood to our children.

In this learning and growing process, as a son in a relationship with the Father, we need to understand there can be hindrances and barriers that need to be removed to experience true sonship. If there are hurts, wounds, and ungodly mindsets and images you have of yourself, with fathers or with God, you must allow God to heal your heart (of any rejection, any fears and insecurities) and address any areas of unforgiveness by the power of His love and healing presence. You must be renewed in your mind by His Word and voice so you can see yourself as a loved and accepted son right before Him, so you can receive all that He has for you as a loving son; so you can learn, be transformed, and live as a true son of God and a godly father.

We also need to understand the impact and effects of sin in our lives and children's lives, and the spiritual warfare we face against a kingdom of darkness, which seeks to destroy individuals, marriages, and families. These realities can contribute significantly to the incredible challenges to godly fatherhood and raising up godly children. This is why Apostle Paul, in his letter to the Ephesians, after teaching how we are to walk as children of light in human relationships, emphatically concludes his letter on teaching them about the spiritual warfare we will face. A final word: Be strong in the Lord and in His mighty power. *"Put on all of God's armor so that you will be able to stand firm against all strategies of the devil. For we are not fighting against flesh-and-blood enemies, but against evil rulers and authorities of the unseen world, against mighty powers in this dark world, and against evil spirits in the heavenly places"* Ephesians 6:11-12 (NLT).

Why this final word with great emphasis? It is because we face a very real spiritual battle with an enemy—Satan and his kingdom of darkness, who seeks to steal, kill, and destroy, with one of their main areas of attack being against the family. The good news is God has given us spiritual armor and weapons as a son of God and father in Christ, and by the power of His Spirit, we can stand strong to resist and overcome all of the assaults from our spiritual enemies that come against our life and our family.

Godly fatherhood is an incredible responsibility with its many facets, tasks, challenges, and the spiritual warfare we face with the spirit of this world and the kingdom of darkness. It cannot be handled in our own wisdom, abilities, and strength, nor solely in the natural realm. It cannot happen successfully apart from knowing God as Father and being a true son, understanding the spiritual realm and reality of spiritual warfare. We need to receive His love, grace, truth, wisdom, power, and anointing daily. We have to be continually filled with His Spirit and be led by it in our fatherhood to meet the challenges, overcome the flesh, sin, and the assaults that come from the kingdom of darkness against ourselves, wives, and children.

So, how do we become and live as true sons of Father God? Here are some foundational truths and relational aspects of living as a son with the Father:

The first step, if you have not done so, is to genuinely give your life to Christ or rededicate your life to Him, if you are not genuinely living for Him. He is the only way and one with the Father. A true son is one who not only receives Jesus as his savior but also his Lord. He is one who is dedicated to loving, following, and becoming like Christ, who is the express image of the Father:

> *"Anyone who receives you receives Me (Jesus), and anyone who receives Me receives the Father who sent Me"* Matthew 10:40 (NLT).

> *"Whoever confesses the Son has the Father also. Let what you heard from the beginning abide in you. If what you heard from the beginning abides in you, then you too will abide in the Son and in the Father"* 1 John 2:23-24 (ESV).

A son lives a lifestyle of spending time in relationship with the Father through worship. God, the Father, inhabits the worship and praises of His children. The Father seeks true sons who will worship Him because of His great love, care, and passionate desire to pour Himself into them. Through worship, He fills us with His presence and all that He is. In His presence, we are filled with His incredible love, peace, and joy. If there are hurts, wounds, or pain, His presence releases healing and freedom to us. In His presence, we can see and know Him as He really is, talk with Him, learn from Him, and experience transformation to become like Him and reflect

Him. The more we spend time with Him as a true son, the more we can become and live like Him as a father.

I love to begin my morning with worship on the way to work or when I first arrive in my office by listening and singing to some of my favorite worship songs; the songs that are really speaking to me or what I want to express to Father God in these times I am with Him. This helps me keep my focus on Him and fills me with His presence, to lead and guide me in my decisions throughout the day and to reflect Him as His son. I also love to lift up worship to Him each night before going to bed by giving Him thanks and praise with my words for all that He is to my family and me, for my life, and all that was accomplished and experienced in the day. Worship and praise do not have to be just with singing songs or listening to worship music, it can be through an attitude of worship from your heart, and expressed with your devotion and words onto God:

> *"But the hour is coming, and is now here, when the true worshipers will worship the Father in Spirit and truth, for the Father is seeking such people to worship Him"* John 4:23 (ESV).

> *"Be filled with the Spirit, speaking to one another with psalms, hymns, and songs from the Spirit. Sing and make music from your heart to the Lord, always giving thanks to God the Father for everything, in the name of our Lord Jesus Christ"* Ephesians 5:18-20 (NIV).

> *"Now the Lord is the Spirit, and where the Spirit of the Lord is, there is freedom. And we all, with unveiled face, beholding the glory of the Lord, are being transformed into the same image*

from one degree of glory to another" 2 Corinthians 3:17-18 (ESV).

A son lives a lifestyle of prayer. Prayer is communication with God, our Father, and for any relationship to grow rich and become strong, there is regular communication, and as with the closest human family relationships, there is daily communication. The beauty of prayer is that the Father desires to communicate with us daily, hour by hour, moment by moment. In the Gospels, we see Jesus demonstrating this relationship with the Father when He would spend time in prayer with Him in the morning, throughout the day, and in the evening. He invites us into that same relationship with Him and with the Father... Jesus taught us, "when you pray, say *Our Father* in Heaven, hallowed be Your name" (Luke 11:2).

A son lives a lifestyle of abiding in God's Word, in Christ's teaching, obeying and living it out. He understands that the Scriptures and teachings of Christ are the very words of God the Father. They are a revelation of who He is, His truth and ways, and our instructions for living as a son. They are not just words on a page; they are inspired from the very breath of God the Father that gives life. His Words are infused with the power to renew our minds and transform us into sons, just like Him:

> *"Everyone who goes on ahead and does not abide in the teaching of Christ, does not have God. Whoever abides in the teaching has both the Father and the Son"* 2 John 1:9 (ESV).

> *"In that day you will know that I am in my Father, and you in Me, and I in you. *[21]*Whoever has My commandments and*

keeps them, he it is who loves Me. And he who loves Me will be loved by My Father" John 14:20-21 (ESV).

"Every good gift and every perfect gift is from above, coming down from the Father of lights, with whom there is no variation or shadow due to change. Of His own will He brought us forth by the word of truth, that we should be a kind of firstfruits of His creatures" James 1:17-18 (ESV).

A son bears fruit in doing the works of the Father in loving and serving others. If we are living in a true relationship with the Father, He will lead and compel us to do the things He is showing us, what He is doing on the earth, and what He desires to do. As a natural father pours himself into his son and involves him in his work or activities, so does our Heavenly Father delights in involving His sons in doing His works:

"I am the true grapevine, and my Father is the gardener... Remain in Me, and I will remain in you. For a branch cannot produce fruit if it is severed from the vine, and you cannot be fruitful unless you remain in Me. 'Yes, I am the vine; you are the branches. Those who remain in Me, and I in them, will produce much fruit" John 15:1, 4-5 (NLT).

"The words that I say to you I do not speak on My own authority, but the Father who dwells in Me does His works. Believe Me that I am in the Father and the Father is in Me, or else believe on account of the works themselves. "Truly, truly, I say to you, whoever believes in Me will also do the works that I do; and

greater works than these will he do, because I am going to the Father" John 14:10-12 (ESV).

As I've traveled the world, my greatest joy is to reach the unreachable, touch the untouchable, and love the unlovable with the Father's love. The ones whom society throws away or considers as cursed or not valuable to society. One time, I was doing some ministry in Tianjin, China, with a team of short-term missionaries to serve and care for orphans with special needs. Many of the orphans had been abandoned and left for dead or dropped off at the orphanage, never to be seen again by their parents, as they are seen as cursed. While serving at this orphanage in Tianjin, we were told about another orphanage for children with special needs that was about 8 hours away by train in the countryside and were asked if we could visit them.

The only time we could visit was on our rest day on the weekend, so I asked my team if they wanted to visit them. They all said yes, so the day came, and we left as early as we could, taking the first train available. After a long train ride, we arrived at the orphanage, and I'll never forget what I saw and experienced. The orphanage workers came out and said that the children were so happy that we were there and that they had been waiting all day for us to come. So, they took us into the orphanage on the bottom floor, where the children were waiting in cribs all along the hallway. There must have been about twenty cribs with two to three children per crib. The children were all moaning, shaking, jumping up and down, and screaming with joy that somebody had come to visit them, which had never happened. So, I asked the workers, "can they come outside so we can spend some time with them?" They said sure and brought every child outside.

You should have seen the joy on their faces hugging us, playing with us, walking with us hand in hand, and receiving the love and affection we had for them. It was a love fest filled with the Father's love that lasted late into the night until our last chance to catch a train back to where we were staying in Tianjin. This is just one of many experiences I've had around the world that I would have never considered or desired to do. But because Father God had so filled me with His love, I couldn't help but go out as His son and do His works, even in the most uncomfortable situations and darkest of regions of the world. The Father's love in me compels me.

Lastly, becoming and living as a true son to become like the Father, you need to have a spiritual father/fathers in your life. As I introduced in the previous chapter, God's fatherhood is not only manifested through natural godly fathers, but also through spiritual fathers. Spiritual fathers are the ones who will embrace you as a spiritual son to pour out their lives into you. They will nurture and teach you the Word of God, correct in love, and guide you to become a mature son who reflects the heart and life of Christ. A spiritual father is invaluable to growing sons to receive godly counsel and to gain wisdom for living that comes from the Father, as they pour into them all that they have learned and experienced with knowing God the Father. Without a spiritual father or spiritual fathers in your life, you will not become and receive the fullness of what God desires to pour into you, as they are His key instruments to raising up strong spiritual sons and future fathers in His house:

> "I write to you, dear children, because you know the Father. I write to you, fathers, because you know Him who is from the beginning. I write to you, young men, because you are strong,

and the Word of God abides in you, and you have overcome the evil one" 1 John 2:14-15 (NIV).

CHAPTER SUMMARY

1. If men have not had a godly father in their homes, it is not only a great hindrance to knowing and having a deep personal relationship with God as Father, but also a major barrier to knowing how to be a godly father.

2. Men often become like their earthly fathers. If they do not have one, they will become like those modeled by their peers, or whatever they feel fathers should be, based on their thinking and capacity to be a father.

3. One may have a desire and choose to be a godly father, but it does not happen by desire and choice alone. Men must be shown, taught, and mentored on how to function and live like one.

4. Regardless of our upbringing, past or current experiences, we can learn and become the godly fathers that God has created us to be. It's never too late!

5. The only way we can become a godly father like Father God is by first becoming a son of God by receiving Jesus Christ.

6. As a son in a relationship with Father God, we experience who He is, His nature, character, truth, and ways by spending time with Him in His presence daily.

7. There can be hindrances and barriers in your life, such as hurts, emotional wounds, or ungodly mindsets that must be removed to experience true sonship with the Father. And to remove these, you must forgive and allow Father God to heal and renew you.

8. We need to understand the effects and impact of sin in our lives and children's lives, and the reality of spiritual warfare with the kingdom of darkness who seeks to destroy individuals and families.

9. We need to be daily filled with God's Spirit, love, grace, truth, wisdom, power, and anointing to handle our responsibilities and challenges as godly fathers and to resist and overcome the sin and the spiritual warfare we will face against our family.

10. A true son lives a lifestyle of spending time in a relationship with Father God through worship, prayer, abiding in His Word, doing the works of the Father in loving and serving others, and receiving from spiritual fathers in his life.

REFLECTION QUESTIONS

1. What impact has your father, or if you are fatherless, the lack thereof, had on knowing and having a relationship with God personally as your loving Heavenly Father?

2. As a father, what traits of your father are you reflecting in your fatherhood to your children? If you did not have a father, how did that affect the way you view and act as a father?

3. What does it mean to you to become a son of God? What is Father God like to you, and how does He reveal Himself to you?

4. What are some of the ways you can experience Father God and grow in your relationship with Him daily as His son?

5. How can you be a father to your children as Father God is to you as His son?

6. How can you provide a spiritual covering to protect your children from the darkness of this world and spiritual assignments of the enemy?

5

THE CALL AND ROLE OF GODLY
FATHERS IN THE HOME

GOD THE FATHER, OUR MODEL
FOR GODLY FATHERHOOD

"For this reason I kneel before the Father, from whom every family in Heaven and on earth derives its name" Ephesians 3:14-15 (NIV). The word for *family* (Patria) is derived from the Greek word for *father* (Pater). So, through this passage, we understand that God's design is the source of life for every family, and it is the Fatherhood of God.[1] Fathers are to be the source of revealing and reflecting the fatherhood of God to their families. This leads us to understand our roles as fathers by looking to Father God, who is not only the source, but also our perfect model. All that He is as

Father to us as His sons and daughters, we are to be, too, as a father to our sons and daughters. So, let's look at His attributes and who He is to us that gives us a picture of our role, responsibilities, and function as a father:

FATHER GOD GIVES US IDENTITY

> *"See what kind of love the Father has given to us, that we should be called children of God; and so we are"* 1 John 3:1 (ESV).

> *"And a voice from Heaven said, "This is My Son, whom I love; with Him I am well pleased."* Matthew 3:17 (NIV).

Every person on the planet has been created with a deep longing to have an identity, to know who they are, and what their purpose is in life. And the greatest identity one can have is to know their true identity, which is that they have been created by God to be His child. The identity of knowing they belong, are known, and are unconditionally loved by Father God. This gives a person great value, significance, and security in their identity, and is the foundation to understand they have been created by Father God for a divine purpose. In Matthew 3:17, we could see that the very first words the Father spoke to His Son, Jesus, before He did one act in His earthly ministry, was to affirm Him in His identity as His son. To affirm that He was loved and that He brought great pleasure to His Father as His Son. The Father's love and pleasure were not based on anything Jesus had accomplished; it was based purely on the fact that He was His Son. This truth of His identity was the foundation that established Him in His life and ministry, knowing who He was and whose He was, and knowing that His Father would always be there with Him throughout His life.

GODLY FATHERS GIVE IDENTITY TO THEIR CHILDREN

As Father God establishes our identity as His children, godly fathers provide identity to their children. They are created in their physical image and likeness, have their DNA and some of their characteristics, and are named with their last name. They are to learn much about who they are through their fathers. Godly fathers are to show them they are unconditionally loved, valued, cared for, and have gifts, talents and abilities. They are to teach, guide, and continually affirm their children with words of encouragement and praise in their identity uniquely made in God's image as their son or daughter that brings them great pride, pleasure, and joy.

FATHER GOD IS LOVING

> *"See what kind of love the Father has given us, that we should be called children of God"* 1 John 3:1 (ESV).

God loves us with an unconditional and perfect love that expresses itself in rich, diverse, and unique ways, whatever is needed for us to feel loved, accepted, safe, secure, and cared for in every situation or circumstance of life.

The apostle Paul's letter to the Corinthian Church gives some of the characteristics of what the Father's love looks like and what we should strive for in reflecting to our children: *"Love is patient, love is kind. It does not envy, it does not boast, it is not proud. It does not dishonor others, it is not self-seeking, it is not easily angered, it keeps no record of wrongs. Love does not delight in evil but rejoices with the truth. It always protects, always trusts, always hopes, always perseveres. Love never fails"* 1 Corinthians 13:4-5 (NIV).

GODLY FATHERS ARE LOVING

Our children were created to be loved, and fathers are to be a primary source of God's love to them. The Scriptures reveal the characteristics and provide us with a picture of God's love, but applying and communicating it to our children is an ongoing learning and fluid process and journey. It's not easy, as we are human, and not perfect as Father God is. We have flaws and weaknesses and are continually working to become like Christ, but God gives us grace and helps us to become the father He's called us to be.

As fathers, we need to understand that each child is created uniquely with their own personality, emotional makeup, and different love languages, which fathers need to learn in order to love and father each child uniquely. This requires adjusting at times, which might not come natural to you, based on how God has made you, your gifts, and spiritual calling. For example, God has made me a strong, intense, apostolic leader, a general in His Kingdom, where I have to be bold as a lion to lead, and strong to carry out the work of the ministry with a mega-church and with my ministry with global missions. I have to be firm to overcome challenges, resolve conflict, and deal with the spiritual warfare that comes with the ministry. These qualities of strength come very natural to me. But I have a teenage son named Ethan, who is a gentle, loving soul and is extremely sensitive. God made him that way. The slightest raise of my voice, feedback, or correction with firmness crushes him and wounds him deeply, even though my instruction or discipline is in love, and has never been out of order or over the top. Because of my makeup as a "lion," what I perceive as a 2-3 level of volume and firmness is received by Ethan at an 8-9 level that hurts him. I've had to learn what my son, Ethan, needs is a lamb, not a lion, as he's in his high teens. The opposite of what I thought was best for him, "firm and tough love," to keep him on track. A bold and firm lion does not work for him, especially in this season of his life. I have to make tons of deposits as a gentle lamb before he can receive loving instruction or correction from a firm lion.

Each stage of our children's childhood, teen years, and transition into adulthood will also require new stages of learning and adjusting, but in each stage, they need to know they are unconditionally loved and accepted. They need to be told, shown, and reaffirmed in your love for them as often as possible as they grow up physically, emotionally, and relationally. Fathers will be a source of strength for them as they face imperfect friends, teachers, and others they come into contact with in a sinful and broken world. If you grew up like me without a father for most of your life or had a father that did not tell you they loved you, or it was said very rarely or never expressed in a meaningful way, this might not come natural to you. But as you grow in your relationship as a son of God and experience Father God's love for you, He will fill your heart with His love, remove what is unnatural or uncomfortable, and impart His desire and expression in you, where saying and expressing it in an authentic and meaningful way to your children will become a natural joy for you.

Loving your children with your words must also be included with actions. Words without loving action will eventually become empty and fruitless.

FATHER GOD IS EVER-PRESENT

"God is our refuge and strength, a very present help in trouble"
Psalm 46:1 (ESV).

"Be strong and courageous. Do not be frightened, and do not be dismayed, for the Lord your God is with you wherever you go" Joshua 1:9 (ESV).

Father God is an omniscient, omnipotent, as well as omnipresent. He has promised to be with us always, even in the midst of our toughest tests, painful trials, and trying wilderness seasons. The Father will never leave us nor forsake us. His loving care is expressed and exemplified in these attributes and teaches us the importance of a father always being available, accessible, and present in their children's lives.

GODLY FATHERS ARE EVER-PRESENT

Being present in the lives of our children as fathers is critical and key. In my own experience as a father, and with the counsel I've often given fathers as a pastor, I strive to and encourage them to invest themselves into whatever their children are interested in, involved in, and love doing. I've found this speaks volumes that you are interested in what they are interested in, care about what they care about, and enjoy spending time with them. This communicates love to them! You spend time with those you love and care about. Watching cartoons and movies they love, playing board games, video games, and sports with them, attending their school, arts, and sporting events, helping them with school work, having meals, and spending as much time with them as possible. A funny example of this; a few years ago, in my late 40s to early 50s, I became skate dad at the skate park, as my teenage son, Ethan, was passionate and active in skateboarding and hanging out at the skate park every day. If I wanted to spend time with him in this season as a mid-older teen, I needed to get creative to invest myself into what he and his friends were into to make sure I could spend some time with him. It was a lot of fun, but a little painful at times, as hitting the concrete with the occasional fall did not feel like it did back in the day when I skated as a kid. But those times were well worth it and gave us lasting memories.

Fathers, to invest time with our kids means getting involved with them in the things that would normally not interest you, nor would you enjoy. But the joy comes with seeing the joy on their faces, knowing that their father loves spending time with them, having fun with them, and is proud to see them enjoy life and thrive in all that they do.

FATHER GOD IS OUR PROVIDER

> *"And my God will supply every need of yours according to His riches in glory in Christ Jesus"* Philippians 4:19 (ESV).

> *"So don't worry about these things, saying, 'What will we eat? What will we drink? What will we wear?' [32] These things dominate the thoughts of unbelievers, but your Heavenly Father already knows all your needs"* Matthew 6:31-33 (NLT).

Countless times throughout the Scriptures, we see God providing for His people. Even when his people complained, when they lost faith, He still held His promise, which continues, even unto us today.

GODLY FATHERS PROVIDE

Just as Father God provides all of our needs as His children, fathers are to also provide for their children. God has created and called fathers to work to provide for their families. They are to provide shelter, food, clothing, and whatever is needed to help their children grow to become successful adults. A godly father accepts this responsibility to care for his family by being a good steward of his gifts, talents, job skills, and pursues opportunities that are available to him to provide. He also takes the lead by working together with his wife to be a good steward of their household finances to ensure the needs of his family will be met.

> *"But if anyone does not provide for his relatives, and especially for members of his household, he has denied the faith and is worse than an unbeliever"* 1 Timothy 5:8 (ESV).

FATHER GOD IS OUR PROTECTOR

> *"Be strong and courageous. Do not be afraid or terrified because of them, for the LORD your God goes with you; He will never leave you nor forsake you"* Deuteronomy 31:6 (NIV).

> *"But the Lord is faithful, and He will strengthen you and protect you from the evil one"* 2 Thessalonians 3:3 (NIV).

God, the Father, is a faithful protector of His children and promises to be with us in every situation and gives us strength and confidence when facing life's challenges, tests, trials, or circumstances that can provoke fear.

Knowing that our Heavenly Father is always with us and is there for us, gives us the security that we will be safe and protected from harm.

GODLY FATHERS PROTECT

In the same way, as Father God is a protector to us, fathers are to be protectors of their children. They provide assurance of safety and security because they are strong and courageous and are always present or available to protect them. As young children, they go to your room to sleep with mom and dad if they've heard something or were awakened by a bad dream that made them fearful. Once they've come into their father's presence, they are able to fall back to sleep and rest without fear. Or if they are with you out in the world and see something that makes them nervous or fearful, they draw closer to their father, knowing he is their protector, and they will be safe. My youngest son, Ethan, who is eighteen, still feels a great sense of safety and security when I'm home. If I'm out at work or out for the evening with my wife or friends, and he's home alone, he'll ask me, "When will you be home? You're not going to be out too late, are you?" Even though he's a young adult and can handle himself as a former martial artist, there is something in his heart that says, I am totally safe and have no fear because dad is home and near to protect me.

As children grow into their teens, fathers are to protect them from ungodly influences and darkness, by teaching them and providing them instruction, guidance, and boundaries. You must love them and care enough for them by asking questions, such as, What are you learning at school? What are you watching on the internet? Where are you going? Who are you going with? What are you guys going to be doing? Why are you getting home so late? Fathers must also love them by warning them of the dangers and consequences of sin, speaking to them in the language that they can hear and receive in a loving and nurturing way. It shouldn't be in an overbearing, harsh, judgmental, or condemning way, in a language that doesn't resonate with them. Our teens will feel they know what's up and can think for themselves, and may even disagree with your counsel or struggle and resist against being told what to do. But, a father must persist in providing this protection, as teens do not have the maturity or discernment to avoid all trouble without instruction, guidance, and godly boundaries.

JESUS IS OUR MODEL FOR GODLY FATHERHOOD

"The Son is the radiance of God's glory and the exact representation of His being, sustaining all things by His powerful Word" Hebrews 1:3 (NIV).

"I have made You known to them, and will continue to make You known in order that the love you have for Me may be in them and that I Myself may be in them" John 17:26 (NIV).

Jesus came to show us the Father in all that He is. The Scriptures say He is the visible image and exact representation of Father God in Heaven. So, looking at Jesus, who He is, and His ministry to us will give us a great understanding of the role and function a father is to fulfill to his children. In the Bible, we see three major offices and ministries that Jesus functioned in—Jesus the Priest, Jesus the Prophet, and Jesus the King. These three main ministries reveal and represent what Fathers are to be to their families.

JESUS AS PRIEST

Jesus, as a priest, was and is our mediator, representing us before God. He offered Himself as a sacrifice for our sins once and for all, and now lives to pray and make intercession for us as our High Priest.

> *"But because Jesus lives forever, His priesthood lasts forever. Therefore He is able, once and forever, to save those who come to God through Him. He lives forever to intercede with God on their behalf"* Hebrews 7:24-25 (NLT).

> *"So then, since we have a great High Priest who has entered Heaven, Jesus the Son of God, let us hold firmly to what we believe. This High Priest of ours understands our weaknesses, for He faced all of the same testings we do, yet He did not sin. So let us come boldly to the throne of our gracious God. There we will receive His mercy, and we will find grace to help us when we need it most"* Hebrews 4:14-16 (NLT).

A GODLY FATHER IS A PRIEST TO HIS FAMILY

Just as Christ serves as a priest to us, a father is to represent his family before God, lifting up prayer and intercession to God on behalf of his children: praying for God's will to be done in their lives, praying for God's protection, grace, favor, and wisdom, and for God to bless all that they put their hands to. If they have committed any sins, for God to forgive and cleanse them, and protect them from evil, ungodly, and corrupt influences. The father has a responsibility to provide a spiritual covering over them, and with this responsibility, God has given fathers the spiritual authority to place a spiritual hedge of protection against the assignments and assaults of the enemy.

We see a powerful picture and principles of a father going to God as a priest on behalf of their children in the life of Job: *"Many years ago, a man named Job lived in the land of Uz. He was a truly good person, who respected God and refused to do evil. Job had seven sons and three daughters.... Job's sons took turns having feasts in their homes, and they always invited their three sisters to join in the eating and drinking. After each feast, Job would send for his children and perform a ceremony, as a way of asking God to forgive them of any wrongs they may have done. He would get up early the next morning and offer a sacrifice for each of them, just in case they had sinned or silently cursed God"* Job 1:1-2, 4-5 (CEV).

Job, as a father, is seen here serving as a priest every morning to sanctify (set apart for God) his kids, by performing a religious ceremony and offering sacrifices for each of his kids to cover their sins. Today's equivalent of the old covenant sacrifices are fathers offering sacrifices of prayer, intercession, thanksgiving and praise for their children. Notice how Job interceded for each of his children because each child is unique. Each child will have different strengths and weaknesses, different struggles and temptations. So, in addition to general prayers according to God's Word and purposes for their life, a father should pray for each of them, specifically according to their unique needs.

In the new testament, we see several situations where it was the father who brought their child to Jesus to receive healing from sickness or freedom from demonic oppression (Mark 9:21-24, John 4:46-54) and through the father, his whole household received salvation:

"Sirs, what must I do to be saved?" They replied, "Believe in the Lord Jesus, and you will be saved—you and your household" Acts 16:30-31 (ESV).

"But As for me and my house, we will serve the LORD!" Joshua 24:15 (ESV).

A father, as a priest, has an incredible responsibility to pray and believe God for the salvation, care, protection, and will of God to be done in the life of his children. And because of this responsibility, God has given the father access to Heaven in prayer, and the spiritual authority in the spirit realm to fulfill his role and ministry to his family.

JESUS AS A PROPHET

"When the people saw the sign that He had done, they said, 'This is indeed the Prophet who is to come into the world!" John 6:14 (ESV).

A prophet is a spokesman for God, one who represents God and speaks His heart, mind, will, and words to God's people. Jesus said of Himself, *"Don't you believe that I am in the Father and the Father is in Me? The words I speak are not My own, but my Father who lives in Me does His work through Me".* Throughout Jesus's life, He represented the Father and spoke the words of the Father that gave life and revealed God's truth and purposes to those He spoke with and discipled.

A GODLY FATHER IS A PROPHET TO HIS FAMILY

In the same way Jesus represents the Father as a prophet to God's children, a godly father is to be a prophet to his family and represent God to his children. He is to speak God's Words of life and truth to his wife and children to build them up, encourage, and strengthen them as they grow up in Christ. He is to speak and teach his children in the instruction and ways of the Lord that equips them for life and their calling. (Deuteronomy 6:5-9, Ephesians 6:4). He is to provide prophetic vision by speaking what the Spirit reveals and what he sees in his children, calling it forth and activating God's prophetic purposes and spiritual gifts in their life.

Proverbs 29:18 reveals to us, *"when there is no prophetic vision we perish and cast off restraint."* If our kids have no prophetic vision or a sense of purpose for their lives, they will have no discipline, run wild, and be without covering. They will become vulnerable to the spirit of this world and the plans of the enemy, who seeks to devour them and prevent them from fulfilling God's purpose for their life. A father has been given the spiritual authority, anointing, and eyes to see what God has created his children for, so he can speak, provide direction, guidance, and train them up in the purposes for which they've been created:

> *"Train up a child in the way he should go; even when he is old he will not depart from it"* Proverbs 22:6 (ESV).

JESUS AS KING

> *"For to us a child is born, to us a Son is given; and the government shall be upon His shoulder, and His name shall be called*

Wonderful Counselor, Mighty God, Everlasting Father, Prince of Peace. Of the increase of His government and of peace there will be no end, on the throne of David and over His kingdom, to establish it and to uphold it with justice and with righteousness from this time forth and forevermore" Isaiah 9:6-7 (ESV).

Jesus is our king, who has a Kingdom that He governs. His Kingdom is established and governed by God's righteousness, peace, and justice. His Kingdom's citizens are made up of God's children, which He cares for and protects from His enemies, ensuring God's will and righteousness for them, which brings security, peace, and joy in their lives.

A GODLY FATHER IS A KING TO HIS FAMILY

In the role of a king, a godly father is to govern and provide leadership to His family to ensure righteousness (what is right before God) and peace in his home. He is to be a servant leader, creating and establishing a culture of godliness in the home that fills it with peace, security, and joy. This includes teaching his children in the instruction of the Lord and Word of God, providing boundaries and discipline to his children in love when needed, to protect them from any ungodly influences or spiritual assignments from the enemy.

A godly father, as a king leading an army in battle, is to be watchful, discerning, and on guard to protect his children from the plans of the enemy. He is to be on the offensive when protecting and leading his family, by using the spiritual weapons of the kingdom—God's Word, prayer, worship, the blood, and authority in the name of Jesus, and calling upon Heaven's armies of angels to keep the enemy at bay.

FOUNDATIONAL CHARACTERISTICS OF A GODLY FATHER

LOVES GOD

> *"And you must love the Lord your God with all your heart, all your soul, and all your strength. And you must commit yourselves wholeheartedly to these commands that I am giving you today"* Deuteronomy 6:5-6 (NLT).

A godly father loves God with all his heart, soul, and strength. He understands that his love for God and wholehearted devotion to follow and be like Him will cause him to be the best father he could ever be to his children. His love for God is demonstrated by spending time with Him daily in His presence, loving Him through personal worship, prayer, studying and obeying His Word, serving Him, and being a good steward to all that God entrusts him with.

LOVES HIS FAMILY

> *"Husbands, love your wives, just as Christ loved the Church and gave Himself up for her"* Ephesians 5:25 (ESV).

> *"Fathers, do not provoke your children to anger, but bring them up in the discipline and instruction of the Lord"* Ephesians 6:4 (ESV).

A godly father loves his wife with all his heart, strength, and care to serve, honor, and bless her as his most treasured gift from God, his lover, best friend, and mother to his children. By loving his wife as God has called him to, he also loves his children and models to his sons and daughters what a godly husband and father should be.

A godly father loves his children by serving, providing for, caring, and protecting them. He spends time with them as a top priority, making sure he's fully present with them relationally and emotionally, not just physically. He spends time with them not just in the home but blesses them by initiating going to places and participating in activities that his wife and children enjoy.

LOVES OTHERS

> *"A new command I give you: Love one another. As I have loved you, so you must love one another"* John 13:34 (NIV).

> *"If anyone says, 'I love God,' and hates his brother, he is a liar; for he who does not love his brother whom he has seen cannot love God whom he has not seen"* 1 John 4:20 (ESV).

> *"Love the Lord your God.... 'Love your neighbor as yourself"* Luke 10:27 (NIV).

A godly father loves God by loving others. This is part of who he is, a son, servant, and friend of God. He has a genuine love for people and seeks to build up, serve, and meet the needs of others who are in his circles of life. A godly father teaches and models loving God to his children by loving others with actions and deeds that reflect the nature, heart, and love of Father God.

LEADS AND TEACHES HIS FAMILY

> *"As for me and my house, we will serve the Lord"* Joshua 24:15 (ESV).

> *"For if he's unable to properly lead his own household well, how could he properly lead God's household?"* 1 Timothy 3:5 (TPT).

A godly father is a servant leader to his wife and children. He provides leadership in all aspects of their lives to ensure they are cared for, protected, thrive, and succeed in all that they do. He serves as the spiritual leader to his children to help them grow spiritually as followers of Christ, modeling and teaching them God's Word, teaching and leading them in spiritual habits of worship, prayer, and seeking God's will and purposes in every area of their lives as they grow into mature young godly men and women:

> *"Love the Lord your God with all your heart and with all your soul. Love Him with all your strength. The commandments I give you today must be in your hearts. Make sure your children learn them. Talk about them when you are at home. Talk about them when you walk along the road. Speak about them when you go to bed"* Deuteronomy 6:5-7 (NIRV).

This passage of Scripture shows us that fathers have the responsibility of teaching their children how to love God with all their hearts and life, and to teach them God's truth and ways, as you experience and go through life with them. It is to be part of the culture and life of your home as a family. I love the truth of these Scriptures because it shows us it is to be organic and relational as you do life together. It doesn't mean having Bible studies and attending church every day or all day long, but taking normal everyday life activities and experiences as opportunities to teach God's truth and principles for living.

A ROLE MODEL TO HIS CHILDREN

> *"For I became your father in Christ Jesus when I preached the Good News to you. So I urge you to imitate me"* 1 Corinthians 4:15-16 (NLT).

> *"Follow my example, as I follow the example of Christ"* 1 Corinthians 11:1 (NIV).

A godly father understands he's a role model for his children and leads them by example. Whatever he does, good or bad, and shows to be permissible, his children will do. This is why it is vitally important for godly fathers to know God's nature, heart, truth, will, and ways, and contend to reflect Father God and Christ in all that they do. Loving God, loving, honoring, cherishing, and serving his wife, loving, caring, protecting, and being a spiritual father to his children, loving and serving others, walking in the light of Christ and Word of God, and hating evil and resisting sin, darkness, and the spirit of this world.

Our children are always watching and will do what they've seen and have learned from their fathers throughout their childhood and teen years. The characteristics, traits, and behaviors that are modeled to them by their father will also continue to be seen in them in their adult life and as parents themselves. Understanding the fruit of fatherhood, godly fathers take their role and responsibility seriously before God. They are passionate to model and impart God's nature, character, and ways to their kids in order to set them up to succeed in life and to multiply godly families and legacy from their lineage, for God's Kingdom.

> *"You, however, have followed my teaching, my conduct, my aim in life, my faith, my patience, my love, my steadfastness, my persecutions and sufferings that happened to me at Antioch, at Iconium, and at Lystra—which persecutions I endured; yet from them all the Lord rescued me"* 2 Timothy 3:10-11 (ESV).

FOLLOWS THE LEADING OF THE HOLY SPIRIT

> *"And I will ask the Father, and He will give you another Helper, to be with you forever, even the Spirit of truth... You know Him, for He dwells with you and will be in you"* John 14:16-17 (ESV).

> *"For as many as are led by the Spirit of God, these are sons of God"* Romans 8:14 (NKJV).

A godly father understands that the tremendous responsibility, role, and tasks that come with being a father and raising up godly kids are not easy. It can be very challenging, difficult, and hard at times, especially during the teen years. He knows there are ongoing natural challenges in every stage of his kids' lives, the reality of sin and temptations to compromise, and the spiritual warfare that exists with the kingdom of darkness. Therefore, he cannot be successful in his own strength, wisdom, and understanding. He needs help from the Holy Spirit. He needs His grace, wisdom, guidance, and direction, especially with tough decisions, or in times of great trial or crisis. Godly fathers cultivate a deep personal relationship with the Holy Spirit so they can know and follow His voice and receive His ministry to them and through them *"so that the fruit of the Holy Spirit: love, joy, peace, patience, kindness, goodness, faithfulness, gentleness and self-control"* will be in them to father their children" (Galatians 5:22).

BEST PRACTICES FROM A FEW GODLY FATHERS (Friends of Mine)

Jeff Kenny

1. I give them my time. Children spell love, not l-o-v-e, but t-i-m-e. They want our presence, p-r-e-s-e-n-c-e, more than they want our presents, p-r-e-s-e-n-t-s. We attended every little league baseball game (and practices), and gymnastics events. I drove them to school every day and picked them up. Most vacations were with our children. When they were young, we'd do a practice each night for a drive through Wendy's for a Frosty. We often made what we called "fast-food-row" dinner trips, where they could order anything from one of the 8-10 fast-food restaurants (we still do that with them today, in their 20's).

2. I give their mother my time. Missy is still my best friend. No mar-riage is perfect; every marriage is challenged. After all, men are from Mars, and women are from Venus. But children need to see that God is first, the marriage is next, and then comes the children. Missy & I have 24-hour get-a-ways often. We take a trip to Half Moon Bay or Monterey. We live in the Bay Area, so we're close to Napa, Lake Tahoe, and any number of places within a couple of hours.

3. I give the Lord my time. After pastoring for 26 years, the Lord gave us new assignments. Missy works for Options Health, a non-profit for women in crisis with unwanted or unexpected pregnancies. My assignment, on the other hand, is in the marketplace as a realtor and property manager. It's still my practice to read through the Bible each year and give the Lord the first part of my day in prayer and devotion.

4. I give myself alone time. That's an important practice to model to our kids. Richard Exley, in his book "A Balanced Life", taught me to balance these four things: work, rest, play, and worship. Time alone is important. I'm a people person and love to be around others, so it's an effort to get away by myself. But, time in the yard, in the pool, reading a book, and other "alone" times are valuable.

Anthony Dorris

1. When my kids were born, I decided to make the altar in my house at their bedsides. I pray and read the Scripture to my kids before they go to bed. It's a practice that has instilled in them the trust and comfort they find in the Word of God. They know to call on God

when they are afraid, confused, or worried about something. They know that their dad can help them by going to God on their behalf!

2. My wife and I have created a culture of prayer in our home; we pray before bed, we pray before school, we pray for healing when we are sick, we pray for our food, we pray for our future! Prayer is the foundation of everything we do!

3. I try to be intentional about spending time individually with each of my children. They are different people that have different calls on their lives and need different kinds of instructions and attention. It gives me a chance to speak into their lives, but more importantly, it helps us get to know one another. I want to know who my kids are, and I want them to know me. This also gives us chances to make lasting memories that only the two of us share; we both look forward to having our time together.

Simeon Plyler

1. The most valuable seed I sowed into my kids' lives was the seed of quality time. I spent my free time with them. I was a coach, a teacher, and a friend. I was going through some old handmade cards my kids made for me when they were much younger. Among them, I found a thank you card my daughter, Amanda, gave me after a field trip when she was in junior high school. As I recall the trip itself, I believe I was the only male figure in the group. My trip with Amanda and her classmates was a success in so many ways. I connected with her and her friends, and as a sign of appreciation, she wrote me a thank you card. It was a keeper. Amanda wrote, "Dad, thank you so much for coming to the Science and History

Museum with us. Even though you were not normal, I enjoyed your company! Please, come with us to our next field trip! I hope you enjoyed yourself. Thank you again for everything!"

2. I believe it is vital for children to have an interested and attentive father, a dad who invests in their lives. I recently realized that investing in my kids was not about spending money on them. I came to understand the nature of God's economy, where I had to use a different kind of tender. I had to respond from my heart.

3. I planted a seed with my daughter when she was young. To build our relationship, we had daddy-daughter dates. I knew this was important. When my daughter was a preteen, we made a deal. We had talked about dating and the purpose of dating. For a lot of people in the world, and I was among them, dating was a social activity. I came to realize dating is the process God uses to help men and women determine if they should be life-long companions in marriage. God's heart is to protect His people, and sex before marriage should never be the basis for a lifetime decision, but often is. It was important to my wife and me, and our daughter understood God would use me as His covering for her. Among my fatherly duties, I recognized I was a protector of her purity.

All these men have walked beside me in our journeys of being and growing as spiritual fathers, and each of them has continually shown me the kind of godly fatherhood that God desires and expresses through his fathers.

CHAPTER SUMMARY

1. We understand our roles as godly fathers by looking to Father God, who not only is the source of godly fatherhood, but our perfect model.

2. Father God gives us the true and greatest identity one can have, which is to know you are His child, unconditionally loved, accepted, and known by Him.

3. As Father God gives identity to us as His children, godly fathers, in turn, give identity to their children.

4. Godly fathers teach, guide, and continually affirm their children that they are uniquely made in God's image, are loved, valued, and have gifts, talents, and a divine purpose.

5. In the same way Father God is loving, ever-present, provides, and protects us as His children, godly fathers are to also be to their children.

6. Jesus being one with the Father is also our model for godly fatherhood. He functioned in three major offices and ministries (as a Priest, Prophet, and King) that reveal and represent what fathers are to be to their families.

7. A godly father is to be a priest to his family, representing his family before God lifting up prayer, intercession, and thanksgiving on behalf of his wife and children.

8. A godly father prays for God's will, provision, forgiveness, and protection to be upon his children. He is responsible and has the spiritual authority to provide a spiritual covering over them.

9. A godly father is to be a prophet to his family. He is to teach them God's Word, truth, and speak God's prophetic vision and purposes he sees for their lives. He is to activate and guide them to grow in their spiritual gifts and talents to equip them for their life's purpose.

10. A godly father is to be a king to his family by providing leadership with creating a culture to ensure God's righteousness, peace, and joy in their home.

11. Foundational characteristics of a godly father are: Loves God, Loves his family, Loves others, Leads and teaches his family, Role model to his children, and Follows the leading of the Holy Spirit.

REFLECTION QUESTIONS

1. Do you truly know in your heart your identity as God's child? What does that mean to you?

2. How have you, as a father, given identity to your children? What are some things you can do to affirm your children in how God has made them?

3. How can you encourage and guide your children to develop their gifts, talents, and abilities?

4. In learning how Father God is our model for godly fatherhood, what are some areas you feel you are doing well? What areas do you need to develop and grow in? What practical steps can you take?

5. As a father, how are you serving your family as a priest, prophet, and king? What specific things can you do to grow in these roles to better serve, bless, and protect your children?

6. What godly characteristics do you feel you have as a father? What characteristics and qualities would you like to develop, and what steps can you take to develop them?

6

THE CALL AND ROLE OF SPIRITUAL FATHERS IN THE CHURCH

L et me begin with some words about spiritual fathers from a spiritual father, "Tony", whom God brought into my life about twelve years ago: "One of the most satisfying and rewarding parts of my life is my opportunity to be a spiritual father to men in every age, ethnic and economic group in the Church and beyond. The need for spiritual fathers among men in the Church is in a crisis state. The breakdown of the nuclear family in the United States, over the past hundred years, has greatly contributed to a similar breakdown in the Body of Christ.

One does not need an "official" ministry designation to minister as a Spiritual Father. The only requirement is that we recognize the need and make ourselves available. In my own personal experience, I have found that listening deeply to another man's heart without judgment or condemnation and with a desire to be available to support and encourage other men will open the flood gates of men who seek to be mentored, encouraged and fathered.

My most important ministry after seeking the living God and ministering to my wife and family is my ministry as a spiritual father. I have involved myself in the men's ministry at my church, with the specific goal of supporting, encouraging and mentoring men as a spiritual father. I only have to be willing to listen…*listen profoundly*…to a man and show genuine love, interest and concern for his life. The opportunity to provide a spiritual father relationship to other men, wherein I can lead a man to seriously consider applying the Word of God to their life, is so abundant! Other men of all age groups seek me out as a spiritual father from outside the church, as I have an opportunity to again…*listen* to their hearts in a family gathering, in business and work gatherings, and in my world as an attorney, as I communicate with men in many different settings and circumstances. As my heart has led me to seek to be a spiritual father to other men, the Holy Spirit constantly draws men from every walk of life and in various settings to seek out that ministry. Loving, caring and listening to other men is the light that attracts them. Spiritual fathering is very practical and not mysterious in the least. In my opinion, it should be a part of the ministry of every mature Christian man.

The opportunities will constantly present themselves to you as your heart leads you to a ministry of spiritual fatherhood. The most important assets of a spiritual father is to understand how our Father God loves us and exercise His love through us to the men who come seeking a spiritual father who will listen, withhold condemnation and judgment, and listen profoundly, doing so over coffee, a meal, or just a long walk together where we can have communication. Practicing spiritual fatherhood is a natural outflow of the presence of the living God in our lives as the Holy Spirit leads and guides us to be spiritual fathers to the many sons that await an opportunity to be loved, listened to and nurtured in the Word of God. The ministry of spiritual fatherhood is most profound and needed now more than ever in our churches."

THE FATHER'S CALL TO TURN THE HEARTS OF THE FATHERS

In the last book of the Old Testament, Malachi, the prophet Malachi gives this prophecy: *"Behold, I will send you Elijah the prophet before the coming of the great and dreadful day of the Lord. And he will turn the hearts of the fathers to the children, And the hearts of the children to their fathers, Lest I come and strike the earth with a curse"* Malachi 4:5-6 (NKJV). In this prophecy, we see a couple of truths: the hearts of fathers on earth have turned away from their sons and daughters, resulting in their children's hearts turning away from them, too. And if fathers don't return to God's order and purpose for fatherhood, we would see a curse on the earth. As I've written in chapter one, the massive epidemic and consequences of fatherlessness we see throughout societies around the world are clear evidence of the curse today.

The other powerful truth is, it is Father God who is initiating the restoration back to His order and purpose for fatherhood. If restored, it will remove the curse and its consequences. He is sending His Spirit (manifested through the spirit of Elijah) to turn the hearts of the fathers first to the children, which would result in the children's hearts turning toward them. As I've written in the previous chapters, God's design and purpose for fathers was not just for biological fathers to produce children alongside the natural responsibilities that come with it, but to be spiritual fathers to reveal and reflect the fatherhood of God to the children in their homes and communities. So, the restoration God is calling for is spiritual fatherhood!

The original language of these Bible verses is referring to *spiritual fathers* and *spiritual children*, biological and non-biological. The fathers back in the days of Malachi have abandoned their role and responsibilities to be spiritual fathers. And tragically, throughout church history, and even more so in many of our churches today, the order and role of spiritual fatherhood is not fully understood or functioning as God intended, or it is not a priority or part of the model and ministry of most churches. The development and multiplication of true spiritual fathers in our churches are not taking place, or it is few and far between. What the apostle, Paul, wrote in his letter to the Corinthians still rings true and even greater today: *"For though you might have ten thousand instructors in Christ, yet you do not have many fathers; for in Christ Jesus I have begotten you through the Gospel"* 1 Corinthians 4:15 (NKJV).

THE WOUNDS OF THE SONS AND VOID OF TRUE SPIRITUAL FATHERS

In the churches I was a part of in my first twelve years as a believer, and in my early years as a minister and volunteer pastor of a local church, there was not much said or taught on the role of spiritual fathers; maybe a sermon or two throughout the year. The message and model of the church was that the senior pastor was the father of the house, and he provided fatherhood through his preaching and teaching. There was no real personal relationship with him! You were a member of his congregation, and if you happen to serve in the ministry or on staff as an assistant or associate pastor, you served as a volunteer or an employee for his purposes and ministry plans to care for the people to grow his church and build his ministry. You were not a spiritual son nor a young or fellow spiritual father of the house.

Even though I was a faithful and loyal servant beyond a fault, there was no personal relationship as a spiritual son or friend. The relationships I had with these men were one-sided. I can count on one hand the number of times I had personal phone calls, coffee, or meals with them one on one or with a few others, and it only happened when they needed to talk about their vision and church business. I don't share this to shame or condemn these men; they were not fathered themselves, leaving them with wounds, insecurities, and lack of understanding of true spiritual fatherhood. They didn't understand the need for releasing other spiritual fathers or raising up spiritual fathers in the house. They were only operating by what was modeled to them in pastoring a church and how to build what they perceived was a successful ministry.

Tragically, many believers and ministers in our nation and around the world share similar experiences to what I've experienced. I've seen, firsthand, the void and lack of spiritual fathers in churches around the world and heard the cries for true spiritual fathers to arise. I've preached and taught on spiritual fatherhood from many pulpits and at many pastors conferences. I can honestly say there has not been one time where I did not have a large number of men, pastors, and ministry leaders comment during the conferences or come up to me afterward to share about their experiences from the effects of dysfunctional church fatherhood and void of true spiritual fathers. Many of them were confused, wounded, hurt, and felt used and abused. Others shared about the obstacles, jealousies, and rejection they've experienced if they felt called to start a ministry or pastor their own church.

At one conference in Kenya with several hundred pastors, I was told by many of the pastors that if an emerging minister, ministry leader, or pastor felt called to start and pastor his own church, he was greatly resisted or rejected. It was seen as an attempt to take away members from the church of the bishop or pastor he was serving. If he eventually moves on to fulfill the call of God on his life, he gets rejected by the fathers of the denomination and church and spoken against. In the Congo, I spoke at a conference of two thousand pastors, ministry leaders, and church workers on spiritual fatherhood. And I was told by the pastor who hosted the conference that there are much jealousy and competition among the denominational bishops and pastors of the city.

He himself was secretly poisoned because he was a threat as a pastor of a rapidly growing church in the city. By God's grace, he survived, but was gravely ill for six months. Having spoken at pastors and ministry conferences in Latin America, Asia, Europe, and the Middle East, I found that control, jealousy, and competition among denominational and church leadership and pastors existed there, as well. I could give many more examples that I've seen and heard of in U.S. churches of the effects and void of true spiritual fatherhood, but I think you've gotten the picture.

This reality in many of our churches is why I believe the Spirit of God with the Father's heart and burden compelled me to write this book. Father God is calling His Church to restore His divine order of spiritual fatherhood, to call pastors and men in our churches to become spiritual fathers, to come forth, be equipped, and arise!

For us to be restored to God's order, design, and purposes for spiritual fatherhood in Christ's Church, we need to get real and not be afraid to uncover the problems and obstacles to true spiritual fatherhood. We've all heard these expressions: "you can't fix what you can't see" or "the first step in solving any problem is recognizing that there is one." We need to take an honest look at our Church models, structures, and models of pastoral leadership that have been flawed or not conducive for what God desires and calls His Church fathers to:

ABSENTEE SPIRITUAL FATHERS

One of the main issues I've seen in denominations and in today's apostolic church networks and churches that has created a culture of absentee spiritual fatherhood is that their models of church function more like a business. This is especially in many of the large, mega, and multi-site campus churches. A business provides services, programs, and products for their customers with the goals to obtain and service as many customers as possible, and to expand to more locations as soon and wherever they can to reach more customers. In this model, there is a brand and a central figure (personality), who represents the brand. In these churches, the central figure is the senior or lead teaching pastor of a church with a staff and volunteer team that provides ministry services, programs, and products (books, teaching resources, ministry conferences, merchandise, etc.) for their church members.

Dr. Mark Hanby in his classic book, *You Have Not Many Fathers,* shares a similar view from his experiences as a pastor, teacher, and national church conference speaker: "Today, a local church will associate with a large ministry or its denominational headquarters and serve as a franchise representative of that well-known product line. The local church receives its name, its logo, and its organizational security by attaching itself to a nationally known 'chain.' Pastors become CEOs of these local run outposts that hire assistant managers to perform in specific areas: visitation, music, youth, office administration, etc. The pastor, along with his assistants, helps to recruit and train a volunteer staff to perform programmed tasks. This results in more business and recruitment of new customers who support buildings at better locations. We call this church growth. We call this success. But what does God call it?"[1]

I have relatives and friends as pastors who are on staff in the business-type models of church, and many of them experience no real community or time to be a connected family. Even though they call themselves a church family and strive to become one, the business-type model makes it difficult to authentically and functionally become one. The senior pastor, pastoral, and leadership staff are too busy running church services, ministry programs, doing ministry, handling church business, and having staff meetings, ministry team meetings, etc., that they don't have time to develop and cultivate deep, authentic personal relationships as a genuine family with the people they serve with and serve. The business-type model of church is about running church services and ministry programs focused on church growth and expansion, not on becoming an authentic close-knit family. Therefore, we have many preachers, teachers, directors, and administrators but very little to no true spiritual fathers and mothers in the church, raising up spiritual sons and daughters.

SPIRITUAL PARENTING OR PROGRAMS?

The Kingdom of God is God's family. God's ultimate purpose and intention for the Church, which Jesus called my *Father's House,* is to reveal, reconcile, and connect people to the Father to become His children and to live as the family of God. Because fatherlessness is an epidemic in our nation and world, Christ's Church must model God's intention for family and his fatherhood. God is our Father, and we are His sons and daughters.

Pastors, ministers, and leaders of Christ's Church are called to be spiritual fathers and mothers, to equip and mature God's sons and daughters for His purposes. God's Church was never meant to function as a business, but as a family. What sons and daughters, spiritual babies, spiritual children, spiritual teenagers and young adults need more than anything is spiritual fathers and parenting, not more ministry programs, events, and products. They need spiritual fathers and mothers to invest their lives into them through deep, authentic relationships so they can grow to become mature sons and daughters and fulfill all that God has created them to be.

CONTROLLING, INSECURE, AND JEALOUS FATHERS

Many pastoral fathers in the Church, who were not fathered themselves or had poor models of spiritual fatherhood, often struggle with insecurities and will operate as controlling and insecure fathers. Their identity and self-worth are wrapped up in everyone in the church seeing them as the great mighty man of God, amazing pastor, great spiritual leader, preacher-teacher, prayer warrior, and sole father of the church. Pride often is a weakness or stronghold in their lives and a major blind spot, but it is seen by others as they continually promote themselves and lift themselves up publicly, touting their accomplishments, seeking affirmation and to boost their self-esteem through the praises of men.

Often, they will control their spiritual sons and daughters who are gifted and anointed, as they perceive them as a threat, so they limit their opportunities to grow and minister in their church. The ministry of their sons and daughters will be very limited in scope and influence and in only what the senior pastoral father sees fit to accomplish his personal vision and agenda for his church. It will not be about empowering, equipping, and activating sons and daughters in their gifts and callings for the Kingdom of God, but using them to build their personal ministry kingdoms. Their sons and daughters are servants of the church to be used, not sons and daughters to invest in, to grow, that thrive, shine, and are celebrated.

The senior pastoral fathers will be the only source of major ministry in the church until they retire, pass it on, or move on to bigger and better church pastoral assignments. Many sons and daughters will be greatly wounded by these fathers and leave as bleeding and rebellious sons and daughters looking for love and affirmation from true spiritual fathers with the Father's heart. A father who will believe in them, invest in them, affirm, empower, and release them to serve with their gifts in their high call and ministry for the Kingdom.

SELF-SERVING FATHERS

In the business-type model of churches, absentee fatherhood, controlling, insecure, and jealous fatherhood, the common trait will be self-serving fatherhood. These types of spiritual fathers are all about their own agendas, interests, and personal gain, including the pursuit of abundant financial gain. They do not understand the heart and ministry of a true spiritual father with the Father's heart to expand God's Kingdom through raising up and multiplying mature sons and daughters. Therefore, they are unable to release other spiritual fathers in their churches, nor impart the Father's heart, order, and purpose to raise up men to become spiritual fathers. Men who will, in turn, raise up their own spiritual sons and daughters.

Over the last fifteen years, I've been able to serve alongside a true spiritual father with the Father's heart, who himself experienced what I've experienced, seen, and described above for many years. But he had a great father at home, who was a pastor and true spiritual father to his church family and community for over forty years, who modeled true spiritual fatherhood in the church to him. A true spiritual father in his life was the key to replication and multiplication.

GOD'S ORDER AND PURPOSE
FOR SPIRITUAL FATHERS

Father God has a divine order. He is very methodical and intentional with His divine order and process in all that He has created and does. The Scripture reveals a design and spiritual law of seedtime and harvest, so in all things on the earth, the seed carries the DNA and produces a harvest after its kind. In this design, with human life, the father carries the seed that is implanted in his wife to birth natural children. The father passes on his DNA to his biological children, and as I've shared in the previous chapter, he is to give them an identity, purpose, teach, guide, protect, affirm, impart, and bless them, etc.

In the same way as natural fathers, spiritual fathers carry the seed, impart their spiritual DNA, and provide a similar role and function to their spiritual children. Father God has designed and called spiritual fathers to: give identity, impart spiritual gifting and anointing, prophesy purpose, nurture, teach, train, discipline, guide, and equip their spiritual sons and daughters for life and their Kingdom purpose. They are to raise up their spiritual sons and daughters to full maturity to live like Christ, to expand God's Kingdom, and to multiply God's work and glory on earth as they fulfill their Kingdom assignment. Without the order of true spiritual fatherhood, sons and daughters will remain spiritually immature and not become all that God has created them to be, nor fulfill all that He has destined for them. Ultimately, preventing or limiting God's ordained Kingdom purposes, through them, from taking place on earth.

In chapter 3, I introduced the three classifications of individuals the apostle, John, describes in his letter (1 John) that gives us a picture of the level of spiritual maturity and experience of these individuals. He writes, "*I am writing to you, dear children, because your sins have been forgiven on account of His name. I am writing to you, fathers, because you know Him who is from the beginning. I am writing to you, young men, because you have overcome the evil one. I write to you, dear children, because you know the Father. I write to you, fathers, because you know Him who is from the beginning. I write to you, young men, because you are strong, and the Word of God lives in you, and you have overcome the evil one*" 1 John 2:12-14 (NIV).

The apostle, John, not only reveals the truth that spiritual fathers are to be functioning in Christ's Church, he reveals why they are needed and should be functioning in the Church! Christ's Church will be continually birthing and filled with spiritual children. These children need spiritual fathers to raise them up to become strong and spiritually mature young men and women, and eventually to become spiritual fathers and mothers themselves.

Let's look at these levels of spiritual maturity and development, and some of the characteristics we will see in each stage to establish and reinforce the need, call, and purpose for spiritual fathers in the Church. John mentions three levels, but there is actually another level mentioned in Scripture prior to the child stage, and that is the spiritual infant stage:

SPIRITUAL INFANTS

> *"But I, brothers, could not address you as spiritual people,*
> *but as people of the flesh, as infants in Christ. I fed you with*
> *milk, not solid food, for you were not ready for it. And even*
> *now you are not yet ready, for you are still of the flesh"* 1
> Corinthians 3:1-3 (ESV).

Spiritual infants are still very fleshly, still dealing with or controlled by sins of the flesh and emotions, and live by their soulish senses. Their lives are guided by what they feel and think and not by their spiritual senses or voice of the Holy Spirit. Just as natural infants, spiritual infants are attention-seeking; they don't care who they disturb, or when they disturb them. They can be very needy, and will constantly require your time and attention, or kick up a fuss until they get their needs met. They will make lots of mistakes and messes. They are very needs-driven and will need constant reassurance, encouragement, and affirmation.

None of this is wrong initially, as spiritual infants are living according to what they know, understand, feel, and need. The spiritual infant stage can be a very important learning stage for new and baby believers to learn to depend on God and learn about His love and reassurance, but spiritual babies should not remain in this stage. They are to grow up on to the next stages of spiritual development and maturity. However, without spiritual fathers and mothers in their lives, they can remain spiritual infants for many years. Their growth to the next stage will take much longer, as they will have to feed themselves and try to figure things out on their own. If they are struggling with overcoming sin and pressing on by themselves, they will become extremely vulnerable to completely falling away and back into their old lifestyle before Christ. This is because they lack the spiritual foundations and strength to continue on without the covering, parenting, and care of a spiritual father or mother. They will become wandering spiritual orphans without a home.

In Apostle Paul's letter to the Corinthian Church, he addressed the believers as spiritual infants, due to their fleshly behavior: pride, disunity, comparison, competition, jealousy, sexual sins, etc. However, later in his letter, we see his solution to get them out of their spiritual babyhood. His solution was they needed spiritual fathers to develop and grow and become mature! They had an abundance of teachers and instructors but had no fathers: *"For though you might have ten thousand instructors in Christ, yet you do not have many fathers; for in Christ Jesus I have begotten you through the Gospel. Therefore, I urge you, imitate me. For this reason, I have sent Timothy to you, who is my beloved and faithful son in the Lord, who will remind you of my ways in Christ..."* 1 Corinthians 4:15-17 (NKJV). The apostle, Paul, embraced them as their apostolic spiritual father through leading them to Christ and will continue his fatherhood to them by sending them his spiritual son, Timothy. Timothy, who had become a spiritual father with the spiritual DNA of Paul, will father and teach them to become spiritually mature, to grow to live like their spiritual father, Paul, as he lives like Christ. Paul writes to his children: "Be imitators of me, as I am of Christ" (1 Corinthians 11:1). This would be made possible because of receiving the fatherhood of God through true spiritual fathers, Paul and his son, Timothy.

SPIRITUAL CHILDREN

> "I am writing to you, dear children, because your sins have
> been forgiven on account of His name…" 1 John 2:12 (NIV).

The second stage toward spiritual maturity is the spiritual children stage. While spiritual babies don't know many of the basics of the faith, spiritual children know them but don't fully practice them. They still need instruction in right living and in the importance of walking in love and unity. In this stage, spiritual children are no longer just preoccupied with their own needs, but seek ways to bless and serve others. The downside of the spiritual children stage is their behavior is unpredictable, full of life and light one moment, and can have great moments of glory and freedom, but dark the next – fall back to patterns of sin or bad behavior. They rebel when they don't get their way; they refuse and don't want or appreciate discipline. In this stage, there may be a hidden lifestyle and secret sins. The key to them moving beyond the spiritual children stage is to have meaningful relationships and accountability with true spiritual fathers and mothers.

SPIRITUAL TEENAGERS

The next stage of spiritual maturity is the spiritual teenager stage. Spiritual teenagers have walked with God for some length of time, had experiences with God and know how to do some things, but they are still learning the true nature of Father God, Christ and the Holy Spirit. One characteristic of this stage that is very common is they are wrapped up in their own agenda, ministry, and revelation, and are constantly trying to make a name for themselves. Sometimes, those in this stage carry great anointing and gifting, but they don't have the character and maturity to sustain effectiveness, multiply, and have lasting fruit. One great problem and pitfall at this stage is to be preoccupied with your calling and work at the expense of your personal, intimate relationship with Jesus.

MATURE SON OR DAUGHTER

The final stage of spiritual development and maturity is a mature son or daughter. This is a grown-up child who can be trusted fully by their spiritual parents. There is a consistency of spiritual maturity and fruit of the spirit present in their lives. They've learned how to live by the spirit and voice of God. The Word of God is strong in their lives, and they have victory over the enemy. Instead of serving themselves, they live to serve God and others. They do things because they are right. They have wisdom gained from experience and faithfulness from passing many tests and overcoming trials! Apostle John describes this level of maturity in the passages below:

> *"I am writing to you, young men, because you have overcome*
> *the evil one... I write to you, young men, because you are strong,*
> *and the Word of God lives in you, and you have overcome the*
> *evil one"* 1 John 2:13-14 (ESV).

The stages of spiritual development and maturity I've described reveal the clear and vital need for God's order and purpose for spiritual fathers to be restored and functioning in our churches. God is not satisfied with children! He wants fully grown mature spiritual sons and daughters who are strong in Him, have overcome the enemy, and are fulfilling their Kingdom purpose. This will not take place until we follow His order and design for spiritual fatherhood. It will not happen until true spiritual fathers and mothers arise and take their place in Christ's Church, to raise up spiritual sons and daughters.

Another reality we need to understand is, if true spiritual fatherhood is not restored and functioning as God intends, spiritual babies and children will grow up to become spiritual parents of God's house who are spiritually immature, self-centered, and lack spiritual parenting skills. The reproduction and multiplication of spiritual fatherlessness, spiritually immature children, and dysfunctional and deficient church fatherhood in our churches will continue.

JESUS, OUR MODEL FOR SPIRITUAL FATHERHOOD

God the father, is the source of all godly fatherhood on earth, so as Jesus is our model for godly fatherhood in the home, He is also our model for spiritual fatherhood in His Church and in the family of God. In the Gospels, we see that Jesus was a spiritual father to His disciples as spiritual sons, whom He loved as a natural father loves his children. He discipled them, taught and instructed them, built them up, and corrected them when needed. He modeled and mentored them in living in God's grace and truth, in serving one another and others, and in the ministry by the leading, anointing, and power of the Holy Spirit. He prepared them, affirmed them, imparted His anointing, and empowered them for the work of the ministry they were called and being sent to. He reproduced Himself in them as His spiritual sons to become spiritual fathers themselves like Him that would build and expand God's Kingdom and family on the earth. He was always with them and promised never to leave them nor forsake them until the very end.

"Jesus called out to them and said, 'Come and follow Me, and I will transform you into men who catch people for God" Matthew 4:19 (TPT).

"As the Father has sent Me, even so I am sending you" John 20:21 (ESV).

"Go therefore and make disciples of all the nations, baptizing them in the name of the Father and of the Son and of the Holy Spirit, teaching them to observe all that I have commanded you. And behold, I am with you always, to the end of the age" Matthew 28:19-20 (ESV).

THE ROLE AND CHARACTERISTICS OF A SPIRITUAL FATHER

SELFLESS AND UNCONDITIONAL LOVE

"This is My commandment, that you love one another as I have loved you" (John 15:12).

As spiritual fathers, we must first and foremost, love as Father God and Christ loves us. And because of His great love, Christ came not to be served, but to serve and give His life for us. This sacrificial love is the love spiritual fathers are called to have and give to their spiritual children.

Love is what will qualify and cause a spiritual father to embrace and raise up spiritual sons and daughters by pouring out his life into them. A love that is expressed with time, action, and deeds and not just with words.

A spiritual father's love will be seen in an authentic and committed relationship with his spiritual sons and daughters. It's more than just spending time with them in a teaching setting or Bible study, it's about a lifestyle relationship with them, opening your heart, home, and daily life to them. (One principle to mention here is spiritual fathers should be the ones to father spiritual sons one on one, and spiritual mothers to spiritual daughters one on one. A spiritual father can have a relationship and father spiritual daughters, but it should be in a team dynamic with his wife as a spiritual mother, or in a small group setting with other spiritual sons and daughters).

A spiritual father's love will be selfless and unconditional, so as to reflect the heart of a servant leader to serve his spiritual sons and daughters, purely looking out for their best interest and not his own. He desires the best for them and will do all that he can to help them grow, mature, and fulfill God's purpose for their lives. A true spiritual father is secure in himself as a son of God and father in God's family. Therefore, he is willing to live and pay the price for his spiritual children to create and leave an inheritance for them. His heart is to see his spiritual sons and daughters do more, and have more than they ever had.

TEACHES AND INSTRUCTS

A spiritual father teaches his spiritual sons and daughters the Word of God and instructs them in godly living. We read in the book of 1 John, the description of the spiritual maturity of young men and women in the Lord was they were strong, the word of God lived in them, and they've overcome the evil one (1 John 2:13- 14). This was the result of spiritual fathers in their lives, who taught and instructed them from their knowledge and understanding of the Word of God, and wisdom from their life experience living it out and knowing the Father.

When Apostle Paul told the believers they had thousands of teachers but not many fathers, this gives us insight into the difference of the teaching and impact that comes from a teacher versus the teaching and instruction from a spiritual father. A teacher is primarily concerned with teaching information, wants everything to be right, and is one who comes and goes. A spiritual father has a different perspective. He sees his spiritual sons and daughters as his family in a long-term committed relationship with them. His focus is not just to teach them information, but to lovingly instruct, train, and guide them personally in the way that they should go, in the way that God has created them with their gifts, talents, and his calling and purpose for their lives. His heart and joy is to see his spiritual sons and daughters grow, thrive, and succeed in all that they do. This only happens in a genuine spiritual father to spiritual son/daughter relationship, and never in an impersonal, shallow, or come and go teacher-student relationship.

"Train up a child in the way he should go; even when he is old he will not depart from it" Proverbs 22:6 (ESV).

"The father of a righteous child has great joy; a man who fathers a wise son rejoices in him" Proverbs 23:24 (NIV).

MODELS AND MENTORS

A spiritual father is a model in reflecting and living like Christ, modeling what it looks like to live out the Word and ways of God as a spiritually mature Christ-follower in every area of life, in personal relationships, marriage, family, life's vocation, calling, and ministry, throughout every season of life, the good and the bad. He also is a personal mentor to his spiritual sons and daughters as they are learning, growing, and gaining experience in life and walking in what God is calling them to. In this role, he provides affirmation, encouragement, praise, and constructive input. He provides continual guidance until they become spiritually mature, strong, and successful on their own in what God has given them, entrusts them with, and calls them to.

The apostle, Paul, reveals this principle of being a model and mentor as a spiritual father in his letter and charge to his spiritual son, Timothy: *"But you, Timothy, certainly know what I teach, and how I live, and what my purpose in life is. You know my faith, my patience, my love, and my endurance. You know how much persecution and suffering I have endured. You know all about how I was persecuted in Antioch, Iconium, and Lystra—but the Lord rescued me from all of it. Yes, and everyone who wants to live a godly life in Christ Jesus will suffer persecution. But evil people and impostors will flourish. They will deceive others and will themselves be deceived. But you must remain faithful to the things you have been taught. You know they are true, for you know you can trust those who taught you. You have been taught the holy Scriptures from childhood, and they have given you the wisdom to receive the salvation that comes by trusting in Christ Jesus. All Scripture is inspired by God and is useful to teach us what is true and to make us realize what is wrong in our lives. It corrects us when we are wrong and teaches us to do what is right. God uses it to prepare and equip His people to do every good work."* 2 Timothy 3:10-17 (NLT)

To summarize these passages, Paul, as Timothy's spiritual father, told his spiritual son, Timothy, I have taught you the Word of God and modeled how to live in everything I've experienced with you by my side, an example he should follow in his life, living in, and trusting in the Word of God.

I shared a testimony in chapter two of God's faithfulness to restore a lost son, who became one of my spiritual sons, "Dan". My relationship with him is a great example of a spiritual father-son relationship, where the spiritual father is a model and mentor to their spiritual son. Several months after I led Dan and his wife, Kelly, to Christ, he moved his family to the city where I lived, to attend the church where I was a pastor, and to be closer to my family and me. He had received me as his spiritual father and wanted his family and him to grow and live for Christ. His family became my family.

We became very close, as we talked each day and spent time a few times a week hanging out and discussing the truths of the Word of God, teachings of Christ, and life with the Holy Spirit. We did this over coffee, meals, working out in my garage, and hanging out in my living room watching sports and UFC. It was very organic and relational. In addition to the things of God, we talked about his marriage, parenting, work, pursuits, and dreams for his life and family. Through this close spiritual father-son relationship, I was a model and mentor to him, providing direction, biblical and practical guidance whenever he needed it or asked for it. This resulted in tremendous spiritual growth and things turning around for him and his family, and he received the blessings, provision, and promises of God.

This relationship continues to this day; however, he's no longer a spiritual child or teenager. He's spiritually mature and strong in the Lord, and a spiritual father himself, not only with raising up his natural sons and daughters, but to other new and young believers whom God has brought into his life.

DISCIPLINES AND CORRECTS IN LOVE

"For the Lord disciplines the one He loves, and chastises every son whom He receives" Hebrews 12:6 (NIV).

"Those who spare the rod of discipline hate their children. Those who love their children care enough to discipline them" Proverbs 13:24 (NLT).

A spiritual father, may at times, need to give correction or discipline to a spiritual son or daughter. If they are in error or have fallen into sin, you must love them enough to correct them and provide accountability to living right before God. As a spiritual father, your heart is to protect them from harm or going off track. A mature spiritual father will correct them with love, gentleness, and in a spirit of humility, knowing that they themselves are far from perfect. They must be quick to forgive their spiritual sons and daughters, affirm that they believe in them, and restore them to moving forward in their spiritual development and call, just as our Heavenly Father does with us.

A spiritual son or daughter will receive correction from a true spiritual father because he has demonstrated his love and care for them through a committed relationship. They will know in their hearts that their spiritual father seeks their best interest to grow and prosper in their life and calling.

It's important to understand that a spiritual father must provide safety to their spiritual sons to be open and transparent, to be able to share their insecurities, weaknesses, and fears. They should provide an atmosphere where they can share and grow from their mistakes without feeling shame, or they've fallen short of being a godly and faithful spiritual son.

PRAYS AND PROTECTS

"So he is able to save fully from now throughout eternity, everyone who comes to God through him, because he lives to pray continually for them" Hebrews 7:25 (TPT).

"My little children, for whom I labor in birth again until Christ is formed in you" Galatians 4:19 (NKJV).

Jesus modeled a lifestyle of prayer for His disciples as His children and continues His prayer for us today, showing us prayer as part of the heart and call of a spiritual father. The Scripture, in Hebrews, reveals He lives to pray for us continually! The apostle, Paul, as a spiritual father to the believers of the Churches he birthed and embraced as his spiritual children, labored in much prayer for them. His heart and ultimate objective of his prayers was for his sons and daughters to be transformed into the image of Christ. Picturing the word 'labor' depicts it is hard work that can be strenuous and painful, at times. This describes the lifestyle of prayer that can include heavy burdens, time, sacrifice, perseverance, and spiritual warfare on behalf of your spiritual children. The lifestyle of prayer Jesus has for us as His children, and the objective Paul had for his spiritual children is the same lifestyle of prayer. And it's the ultimate objective of all true spiritual fathers today to see their spiritual sons and daughters become and live like Christ in their lives and high calling.

A spiritual father has a heart and burden to pray and intercede for his spiritual sons and daughters daily. He prays for God's will and purposes to be done in their lives. He prays for God's grace, favor, and anointing to be upon them. He prays for the spirit of wisdom and revelation to be upon them and for God to give them an understanding of God's incredible love for them, His truth, calling, and power in their lives. He prays for God's provision and blessings to be upon them and for God to bless all that they put their hands to. He prays for God's protection to be upon them, and his angels of protection would cover and surround them. In addition to general prayers, in line with God's Word and purposes, he prays specifically for each spiritual son or daughter by the leading and direction of the Holy Spirit, as each one's needs, stages of life, and life's calling are different. The will of God is unique and very different for each of their lives.

The Scripture reveals to us that we don't always know what to pray, but the Holy Spirit helps us with intercession (Romans 8:26). As God's plans and purposes are unique for each one of us, we will not always know His plans for our spiritual sons and daughters, nor understand His process to prepare and mature them. In light of this, one of the best forms of prayer is to pray in the Holy Spirit (spiritual prayer language) and ask the Holy Spirit to show us how and what to pray. The Scriptures teach us to pray continually with the Spirit...

> *"And pray in the Spirit on all occasions with all kinds of prayers and requests. With this in mind, be alert and always keep on praying for all the Lord's people"* Ephesians 6:18 (NIV).

IMPARTS GIFTING, ANOINTING, AND BLESSES

> *"For this reason I remind you to fan into flame the gift of God, which is in you through the laying on of my hands"* 2 Timothy 1:6 (ESV).

"When they had crossed, Elijah said to Elisha, 'Tell me, what can I do for you before I am taken from you?' 'Let me inherit a double portion of your spirit,' Elisha replied" 2 Kings 2:9 (NIV).

The above Scriptures are just a few examples that reveal the truth and role of spiritual fathers to impart to their spiritual sons and daughters. Spiritual fathers have been given the responsibility, spiritual authority, and anointing to impart spiritual gifts, anointings, and blessings upon their spiritual sons and daughters. This comes by prayer, the laying on of hands, and prophecy but in the context and outcome of a spiritual father to spiritual son/daughter relationship over many years. This is God's order and design for spiritual fatherhood to pass on their spiritual DNA and spiritual inheritance.

We see this order and pattern through Scripture, such as with:

- The transfer of prophetic mantle and increase of prophetic anointing from Elijah to Elisha.
- The impartation of leadership and spiritual authority from Moses to Joshua to lead God's people.
- The anointing of the prophet, Samuel, to the prophet-king, David.
- The impartation of apostolic leadership, revelation, and faith from Paul to his spiritual sons, Timothy and Titus.
- The prophet, Agabus, to his four daughters who prophesied.[2]

Going back to what we've learned in chapter three about the prophecy in Malachi 4:16, Father God sent the spirit of Elijah to turn the hearts of the father to the children and hearts of the children to the fathers. Why the spirit of Elijah? Why not the spirit of Moses, David, or one of the other great prophets? If we look at the life of Elijah, we can see that he had the heart of a true father with many prophetic sons. But what's most profound about Prophet Elijah that reveals the purpose and impact of spiritual fatherhood is, he was the only prophet we read about in the Bible that imparted a double portion to a spiritual son. God has sent his spirit (spirit of Elijah) because it's His divine order that spiritual fathers would invest in their spiritual sons and daughters and impart a double portion of their Spirit and anointing.

Spiritual fatherhood is God's design and plan to expand His Kingdom on earth through His sons and daughters, and if we follow His order, we will see a continual increase of God's Kingdom, anointing, glory, and power from generation to generation manifesting on earth.

Spiritual fathers bless their spiritual sons and daughters, speaking words of blessing, edification, affirmation, strengthening, and encouragement. Life and death are in the power of the tongue, and spiritual fathers have an incredible role in blessing their spiritual sons and daughters. This will give them life and strengthen them to accomplish anything they set their hearts to do and hands to. Their words of blessing have the power to tear down discouragement, doubt, unbelief, and any other negative thinking. The power to strengthen and empower them with faith and hope that causes them to persevere and accomplish their goals and overcome any challenges or mountains they face.

In my own life with the many hardships, tests, and trials I've faced over the years in the ministry, and with the lofty goals I've set for myself, there were many times I wanted to give up and throw in the towel!! But I had a spiritual father, "Tony," who called me every day or would meet me for coffee several times throughout the week to check up on me. Each time, it resulted in him blessing me with words of encouragement that infused me with faith and strength to be like Christ, press on, and persevere. It didn't matter what I was going through or how bad it was; he always presented it as the best gift I could receive, seeing it as God's grace and transforming work in my life as a general in God's Kingdom.

There are many other facets and characteristics to spiritual fatherhood that I could share and briefly expound on, but I'm sure you've recognized that the role and function are the same in many ways - as the fatherhood of God is to us as His children, and godly fathers are to their natural children.

Since I've been in the church and ministry, going on thirty years now, I've seen a lot of pastors and ministers' function with the call, passion, and commitment in what I've written to provide spiritual fatherhood to their natural sons and daughters. This has been a blessing to God's Church, as there has been a multiplication of churches and ministries through these natural sons and daughters. I thank God and honor their faithfulness and commitment to their natural sons and daughters. But if we rightly interpret Malachi 4:16 and see how the Church functioned in the New Testament, we would see that God desires and calls His Church fathers to not just raise up their natural sons and daughters, but with the same passion and commitment, to raise up and train spiritual sons and daughters to fulfill their high call and to receive their spiritual inheritance in Christ's Church, to disciple the nations and transform our world.

STRATEGIES AND PRACTICAL MODELS FOR SPIRITUAL FATHERHOOD IN THE CHURCH

1. ADJUST THE VISION AND CULTURE OF THE CHURCH FROM A BUSINESS MODEL TO BEING A CLOSE-KNIT FAMILY

Adjust the model of church services, weekly ministries, and programs for church growth and expansion from a business model of reaching and servicing more people (customers), to a culture of becoming and functioning as a close-knit family with those you serve and serve with, focused on spiritual parenting and raising up and maturing spiritual sons and daughters in all that you do.

(Churches do have to operate as a business or as a non-profit with staffing, budgets, HR, etc., but outside of business administration, the culture of the church and work of the ministry should be in the context of loving, serving, caring, and building close relationships with one another as a close-knit family).

At my church, "Higher Vision", which is a multi-site mega-church, we've adjusted our vision and church ministry models many years ago to be very intentional with the members of our church building relationships with one another in small groups we call "Circles". We've eliminated our mid-week mid to large size ministry gatherings and ministry meetings we called rows and came to understand that circles are better than rows for building close relationships as a family. This resulted in starting and multiplying hundreds of circles for our church family.

Getting connected to a Circle is part of our mission statement, and the DNA of who we are that is imparted to our church family. We strongly encourage everyone to get plugged into a circle. The primary focus of Circles is for our church members to develop relationships with one another as a family and to receive pastoral care (spiritual parenting) from our leaders who are spiritually mature and have the heart to invest in the people they serve. Most churches have small groups for the purposes of creating community and discipleship. However, many are missing the dimension of spiritual fatherhood. They do not have the culture of their small group leaders serving as spiritual fathers and mothers to the people they meet with, serve, and have Bible studies with.

2. SENIOR AND LEAD PASTORS MODEL AND REPRODUCE SPIRITUAL FATHERHOOD

Jared Ming, lead pastor of Higher Vision, provides some great examples of spiritual fatherhood for senior and lead pastors. God led him to identify a handful of men he could meet with weekly to pray with and pour himself into their lives. They call this group "The Wall" to stand in the gap for our church family and for one another in the Wall. They've been meeting for over 10 years that has included connecting with each other by phone throughout the week, playing golf, or meeting over meals.

Jared is also a spiritual father and mentor to our young and new staff and campus pastors. He's investing himself into their lives through committed relationships, meeting with them weekly, and connecting with them throughout the week or when needed to mentor and coach them, and pray for them not, only in their role as church pastors, but also as husbands and fathers to their families, and leaders to their communities.

Often, senior and lead pastors are too busy doing the work of the ministry and caring for their own families that they've not been able to provide spiritual fatherhood to individuals personally. Throughout this chapter, I've presented God's order and purpose for spiritual fathers in the Church. The message is not for senior and lead pastors to become the sole spiritual fathers in the Church by having deep, committed relationships with everyone in their church, or with as many people as possible. That is not realistic, nor is it what Jesus modeled for us. Jesus had thousands of followers and disciples, yet He chose twelve to be His spiritual sons, and even among the twelve, there were three that were especially close to Him.

I believe it is God's heart and call for every senior and lead pastor to not only provide apostolic fatherhood to their church as a whole, but to identify the twelve and the three God's calling them to invest their lives in as a spiritual father to sons and daughters through a real personal and committed relationship. If our senior and lead pastors do not model true spiritual fatherhood, the culture of spiritual fathers serving in our churches, and the mission to raise up and release men to become spiritual fathers, and women to become spiritual mothers will not take place. Senior and lead pastors are the key to impart God's heart, order, and purposes for His fatherhood to take place through spiritual fathers and mothers in the Church.

3. ADJUST THE CULTURE AND ROLE OF THE PASTORAL & LEADERSHIP STAFF TO LEAD AS SPIRITUAL FATHERS AND MOTHERS, NOT JUST AS BOSSES AND SUPERVISORS

Adjust the culture and role of the pastoral and leadership staff to not just provide oversight and direction to their staff and volunteers as their supervisors, but to build authentic personal relationships with them. Get to know them personally, their families, and what's going on in their lives. Embrace the heart and role of a spiritual father, spiritual mother, spiritual big brother and sister with those you serve with, and those you serve.

As an executive pastor with several staff pastors, ministry directors, and support staff that report to me, I'm intentional in getting to know them personally and demonstrate I care for them as a brother and sister with the heart of a spiritual father. They are more than an employee or fellow staff member to me; they are my spiritual family. I provide encouragement, biblical guidance, and pray for them concerning their personal lives, families, things they are in need of, and believing God for. On the professional side of my role as their supervisor, I'm intentional to be a model and mentor in how I lead, direct, coach, and empower my staff, not as their boss, but as a spiritual father and mentor to help them grow, mature, and be successful as young pastors, leaders, and workers for the Kingdom of God.

Spiritual fatherhood can take place in a very real and powerful way among Church staff and volunteers; it's a matter of the culture and model of the church. (Church business model or Kingdom model as God's Family?)

4. **ADJUST YOUR WEEKLY MINISTRY PROGRAMS TO NOT JUST PROVIDE DISCIPLESHIP, COMMUNITY, AND MINISTRY, BUT TO PROVIDE SPIRITUAL FATHERHOOD**

a. Empower and equip the leaders of your weekly ministries, Bible classes, and small groups to be spiritual fathers and mothers to those they meet with and serve.

b. Cultivate a culture of mature believers that are part of these ministry programs, classes, and small groups to become and serve as spiritual fathers and mothers, as well, to others in the church family. God has called every spiritually mature believer to raise up sons and daughters. (1 John 2: 12- 14, Titus 2:3-5)

c. Cultivate the culture of leaders and other mature believers to spending one on one time in a committed relationship with a few new and young believers or in smaller groups outside the weekly ministry meetings, classes, and small groups.

A great example of this is with the Men's ministry in my home church. Randy, our men's pastor, implemented a model where the men would commit to connecting with each other outside of their weekly men's ministry meeting and gather in groups of two or three. The commitment included calling each other daily and meeting, at least, once a week. Randy and his leadership team empowered and assigned men who were spiritually mature to serve as spiritual fathers or mentors to the others in these groups. It has been very effective in building relationships and for our men, who are new and young believers, to grow in their faith and spiritual maturity.

Another great example is through a fellow pastor and friend of mine, "April". She serves as the executive worship pastor with the oversight of the worship ministry and worship teams (musicians and singers) in our church. In her role, she has been very intentional about creating a culture of family and inclusion among the team, as well as making time personally for everyone she leads and serves. She makes sure to connect with everyone weekly, in person, to check on them, encourage and pray for them, as well as connect with them throughout the week over the phone. Her heart is not to just provide direction and instruction to serve well on the worship team, but as a spiritual mother to see them grow and thrive with their gifts and in their calling. She develops a plan for each one of them, goes over books, worship training, devotions, etc., and meets with them weekly to grow as a worship artist and in their identity and walk with Christ. Her heart and goal, as a spiritual mother, is to see her worship spiritual sons and daughters become and live out as spiritually mature sons and daughters of God.

A truth I want to reinforce here is the fatherhood of God flows through both spiritual fathers and spiritual mothers. Although much of the language throughout this book has focused on fathers, the truths, principles, and characteristics of spiritual fatherhood, they can also be applied in the role and function of spiritual mothers to their spiritual sons and daughters.

There are several other strategies and examples of spiritual fatherhood I could share, but I want to challenge you to seek out and learn from other churches and church leaders that are doing a good job with spiritual fatherhood. Also, to develop new strategies and practical models of spiritual fatherhood yourselves. The Spirit of God is calling us and anointing us with His heart and mind. He will show us how we can uniquely provide His fatherhood to the Church families and communities he's entrusted to us. Will you have ears to hear what the Spirit is saying to the churches? Will you respond to the Father's call?

CHAPTER SUMMARY

1. Father God has sent His spirit (spirit of Elijah) on the earth to turn the hearts of the fathers and children, restore His purposes for spiritual fatherhood, and to remove the curse and effects of fatherlessness. (Malachi 4: 5-6).
2. This prophecy and call of Malachi 4: 5-6 is a restoration of spiritual fatherhood.
3. Many believers and ministers in our nation and world have experienced the void of true spiritual fathers and the effects of absentee, controlling, insecure, jealous and self-serving fatherhood in the Church.

4. Churches must shift their models of church and pastoral leadership from a business model to a Kingdom model of God's family. Move from ministry programs to spiritual parenting to raise up and mature spiritual sons and daughters.

5. The Kingdom of God is the family of God. Because fatherlessness is an epidemic in our nation and world, Christ's Church must model God's intention for family and His fatherhood.

6. The Church needs spiritual fathers and mothers to develop and raise up spiritual infants, spiritual children, and spiritual teenagers to become spiritually strong and mature young men and women in the Lord, and future spiritual fathers and mothers.

7. Jesus is our model for spiritual fatherhood. He loved His disciples as spiritual sons. He taught, instructed, corrected, built up, modeled, mentored, prepared, imparted His anointing, and empowered them for life and the work of the ministry they were called to.

8. The role and characteristics of spiritual fatherhood include: selfless and unconditional love; teaches and instructs; models and mentors; disciplines and corrects in love; prays and protects; and imparts gifting, anointing, and blesses.

9. A spiritual father's heart is to see his spiritual sons and daughters thrive and succeed in all that they do, to have and do more than they ever have.

10. Spiritual fatherhood is God's design and plan to expand His Kingdom on the earth through sons and daughters.

REFLECTION QUESTIONS

1. How does the prophecy in Malachi 4:5-6 apply to you as father, mother, son or daughter in God's Kingdom? What are some steps that you can

take in your personal life to be restored to God's order for spiritual fatherhood?

2. Have you experienced absentee, controlling, insecure, jealous, and self-serving fatherhood in the Church? How has it affected you? What steps can you take to receive healing and restoration, and come under true spiritual fatherhood?

3. How can you contribute to your church becoming a close-knit family? How can you become a spiritual father or mother in your church? Ask God to show you new or young believers you could embrace in a committed relationship as a spiritual son or daughter.

4. How does Jesus model spiritual fatherhood to you? What are some things you can emulate?

5. What are some characteristics, as a spiritual father, that you do well? What are some characteristics that you need to develop and put into practice?

6. What spiritual impartation and inheritance do you want to pass on to the natural and spiritual sons and daughters God has given you?

7

THE CALL AND ROLE OF MODERN APOSTOLIC FATHERS

In chapter three, I've provided a biblical foundation to the role and ministry of apostles in the Church today and introduced God's order and design to reveal His fatherhood through apostolic fathers. In the New Testament, we see there were many facets and functions to the ministry of the early Church apostles, such as: missions, preaching the Gospel, Church planting, overseeing Churches, building up the Church, teaching and equipping the saints, etc. In this chapter, I want to highlight how they functioned as apostolic fathers to provide a template for modern-day apostolic fathers. I see two primary realms of apostolic fatherhood in the New Testament: apostolic fathers to Churches and apostolic fathers to spiritual sons and daughters:

APOSTOLIC FATHERS TO CHURCHES

"For though you have countless guides in Christ, you do not have many fathers. For I became your father in Christ Jesus through the Gospel" 1 Corinthians 4:15 (ESV).

"My children, with whom I am again in labor until Christ is formed in you" Galatians 4:19 (NASB).

"For you know that we dealt with each of you as a father deals with his own children, encouraging, comforting and urging you to live lives worthy of God, who calls you into his Kingdom and glory" 1 Thessalonians 2:11-12 (NIV).

Apostle Paul identifies himself as the father of the Corinthian Church in his letter to them, stating that he became their father by leading them to Christ through his preaching of the Gospel, and his intention to continue to father them to become like Christ through sending them his spiritual son, Timothy, an apostolic father who was just like him. We also see the apostle Paul's heart and devotion as an apostolic father to the Churches in Galatia, committing his life in prayer and spiritual travail for them as his spiritual children until they became and lived like Christ. (Galatians 4:19)

In addition to the apostle, Paul, starting and fathering the Corinthian Church and Galatian Churches, many believe he started anywhere from fifteen to twenty Churches. In Asia alone, the New Testament mentions Churches in Ephesus, Smyrna, Pergamum, Thyatira, Sardis, Philadelphia, Laodicea, Colossae, and Hierapolis.

We also see in Scripture that the apostle, John, was an apostolic father to the Churches in Ephesus and throughout Asia Minor, fathering, teaching, and instructing them as his spiritual children. We see his father's heart throughout his letters to these Churches: *"My little children, I am writing these things to you so that you may not sin"* (1 John 2:1); *"Little children, let us love not in word and speech, but in action and truth"* (1 John 3:18); *"I have no greater joy than to hear that my children are walking in the truth"* (3 John 1:4).

APOSTOLIC FATHERS PLANT AND FATHER CHURCHES

So, the foundational role and function of modern apostolic fathers is the planting and fathering of churches (communities of believers), embracing and serving them as his spiritual children. An apostolic father has the Father's heart to father His Church as his spiritual children in a deep, committed relationship. In this relationship, he loves, serves, leads, models Christ-likeness, teaches, equips, guides, provides ongoing care, and prays for them until they become spiritually mature sons and daughters, who reflect and live like Christ. Essentially, providing much of what I've written in chapter six about spiritual fathers with their spiritual sons and daughters, but apostolic fathers provide spiritual fatherhood to their spiritual children (church family) as a whole.

You might be saying the functions I've just shared about apostolic fathers are essentially what most pastors of churches provide, which is true in many cases, but the heart, passion, and personal, relational commitment to see and raise them up as his spiritual children is the key to being an apostolic spiritual father as against just being a typical senior or lead pastor-teacher. Many pastors function more in the capacity the apostle, Paul, was addressing with the Corinthians as "thousands of instructors and guides" (preachers and teachers), but not as spiritual fathers to them as his spiritual children. They have little to no personal relationships outside of preaching and teaching their church members from their pulpits, and shaking hands at the door as they leave. Personally, they are not very accessible nor available, except to those who assist and serve them.

In many churches, the pastor is an employee of the church who is hired by a board to lead a staff, preach, teach, counsel, and perform communion, baptisms, weddings, and funerals for the congregation. He reports to an elder board, and if he does not perform well, according to their standards and expectations, he is voted out and replaced. Short term pastorates and high turnover take place in this church structure and form of church government. Studies show the average stay at a church for a senior pastor is about four years. Youth pastors last about three[1].

In this church system, the pastor is not able to become an apostolic spiritual father to birth and raise up spiritual children, as he sees his church congregation as just that, not as a spiritual family he's deeply relationally committed to long term. The effect goes both ways, as members of a church in this church system do not see themselves as spiritual sons and daughters to the apostolic father and spiritual fathers and mothers of the house. Therefore, they are not deeply relationally committed, either. Leaving a church to find a new church every several years is pretty common, as they do not belong to an apostolic father or to any spiritual fathers and mothers in the church, resulting in stagnancy or setbacks to their spiritual development to become mature sons and daughters of God. The solution to change this reality is to restore God's order and design for apostolic and spiritual fatherhood—*"Turning the hearts of the fathers to the children, and the hearts of the children to their fathers"* (Malachi 4:6).

APOSTOLIC FATHERS PROVIDE VISION AND DIRECTION

In addition to apostolic fathers developing their church family spiritually, they also provide an overall understanding of God's purposes on the earth and hear what the spirit of God is saying to them, as it relates to His church's mission and work. They provide vision and direction to guide their church family to discover and fulfill God's purposes for their lives individually and corporately as a church to reach their city.

Proverbs 29:18 tells us that without vision, the people perish and lack restraint. An individual without a personal vision for God's call upon their life will lack direction and discipline and will wander. They can even be taken out of God's will and purposes for their lives. They will become susceptible to the spirit of this world, and the enemy's plans to keep them from growing spiritually, becoming like Christ, and serving God's Kingdom.

Corporately, if a church family lacks vision for their Kingdom mission and assignment to reach their city, there will be no kingdom alignment, clarity or unity of purpose, and motivation for the ministry to reach out beyond the four walls. The church ministry will be inward-focused, resulting in little to no church growth and impact in their city. Over time, members of the church family will grow discontent and frustrated because they are not being equipped and activated to fulfill their call outside the four walls of the church. This will eventually lead to being critical of the church's vision, mission, and ministries resulting in backbiting against the senior pastor and pastoral leadership. Seeds of discord and division will be sown, causing the church family to remain in a spiritually immature and unhealthy state, and sons and daughters leaving the house.

As I write this, we are in the middle of a global pandemic, Covid-19, nationwide protests concerning racial injustice, systemic racism, police brutality, and a 2020 presidential election cycle (in the USA) that has brought about tremendous fear, confusion, division, and conflict in our nation. Apostolic fathers arise in times like this to hear what the Spirit is saying to the Churches to provide vision and direction, keeping the Church family focused on reflecting Jesus, representing God's truth and righteousness, and doing the works of Christ in our communities.

APOSTOLIC FATHERS ESTABLISH ORDER
AND APPOINT SPIRITUAL LEADERS

Apostolic fathers provide spiritual fatherhood by establishing order in the Church by appointing elders (spiritually mature leaders and shepherds) to help provide spiritual fatherhood and leadership to the Church or Churches under their care and oversight. We see this facet of apostolic fatherhood in the lives of the early Church apostles:

> *"Paul and Barnabas also appointed elders in every Church. With prayer and fasting, they turned the elders over to the care of the Lord, in whom they had put their trust"* Acts 14:23 (NLT).

> *"This is why I left you in Crete, so that you might put what remained into order, and appoint elders in every town as I directed you"* Titus 1:5 (ESV).

Apostolic fathers have tremendous five-fold ministry gifting and capacity to lead, minister, and provide oversight. As a result, they often struggle with delegating and empowering other leaders and can lean toward control or micro-managing. The role of apostolic fathers is to empower and release other leaders to establish order and to ensure effective care and ongoing spiritual growth for the whole Church family. We see a great example of this in the book of Acts with the early Church. They were experiencing explosive growth that resulted in challenges and conflict for the care of all, so the apostles appointed leaders to serve:

> *"In those days when the number of disciples was increasing, the Hellenistic Jews among them complained against the Hebraic Jews because their widows were being overlooked in the daily distribution of food. So the Twelve gathered all the disciples together and said, 'It would not be right for us to neglect the ministry of the Word of God in order to wait on tables. Brothers and sisters, choose seven men from among you who are known to be full of the Spirit and wisdom. We will turn this responsibility over to them and will give our attention to prayer and the ministry of the Word"* Acts 6:1-4 (NIV).

APOSTOLIC FATHERS RELEASE FIVE-FOLD MINISTRY GIFTS

Scripture reveals that Christ Himself gave the gifts of the Apostle, Prophet, Pastor, Teacher, and Evangelist to His Church to equip the saints for the work of the ministry, build up the body of Christ, establish unity of the faith, and bring us to full maturity in Christ (Ephesians 4:11-13). We also know God has placed the apostle first in the Church, meaning first in place and rank in leadership (1 Corinthians 12:28). Apostolic fathers understand the vital importance and need for the five-fold ministry gifts to function in the Church. They are to not only provide ministry; they are to function as fathers and mothers in the house that God's placed them in. They have a ministry gift, anointing, and spiritual impartation they are uniquely designed and anointed for that is needed to equip and mature every member of the Church family.

Apostolic fathers, as the lead apostle and father of the Church, must empower and release the five-fold ministry gifts (fathers and mothers) to serve, build up, and equip the Church family and network of Church families under their oversight. Without the fullness of the five-fold ministry gifts functioning in the Church, God's people will not come to the full maturity in Christ. We will also not experience the full expression of ministry and power in Christ's Church and on the earth that God has purposed and destined.

APOSTOLIC FATHERS TO SPIRITUAL SONS AND DAUGHTERS

I shared in the previous chapters that Jesus is our model for godly fatherhood in the home and model for spiritual fatherhood in the Church. As a spiritual father, Jesus fathered the twelve disciples as spiritual sons to prepare, equip, and empower them for their life's calling and ministry as apostles. In addition to being our perfect example for godly and spiritual fatherhood, Jesus is also our model for apostolic fatherhood. Jesus, among other things, is the Apostle of our faith (Hebrews 3:1).

Apostolic fatherhood is an expression of spiritual fatherhood, but there are a few distinctives from spiritual fathers who are not modern-day apostles. A distinctive I see with Jesus's fatherhood to His spiritual sons was He chose them specifically to become the apostles he would commission to build, expand, and father His Church. He fathered those who had a calling and ministry office He could model, train, mentor, and reproduce Himself in. A ministry office, grace, and anointing that He walked in, and through His spiritual fatherhood would result in an impartation of His apostolic anointing, grace, gifting, and power.

In the life of Apostle Paul, we could see he had spiritual sons that became apostles with his spiritual DNA and provided apostolic spiritual fatherhood to churches under their care: *"To Timothy my true son in the faith: grace, mercy and peace from God the Father and Christ Jesus our Lord"* (1 Timothy 1:2); *"For this reason I have sent to you Timothy, my son whom I love, who is faithful in the Lord. He will remind you of my way of life in Christ Jesus, which agrees with what I teach everywhere in every church"* (1 Corinthians 4:17); *"To Titus, my true son in our common faith: grace and peace from God the Father and Christ Jesus our Savior"* (Titus 1:4).

So, we see through the life of Jesus and the apostle Paul, who are models for apostolic fathers today, that apostolic fatherhood includes raising up and reproducing themselves in their spiritual sons and daughters. They are to equip, empower, and commission them as apostles or in whatever five-fold ministry office they are called to, as fathers and mothers, to serve the body of Christ and to expand God's Kingdom.

CHAPTER SUMMARY

1. The early Church apostles functioned as apostolic fathers to the Churches and provided us a template for modern-day apostolic fathers.

2. There are two primary realms of apostolic fatherhood in the New Testament: Apostolic Fathers to Churches, and Apostolic Fathers to spiritual sons and daughters.

3. The foundational roles of apostolic fathers are to plant and father churches.

4. Apostolic father birth and raise up spiritual children in committed relationships. They see their church as their spiritual children and family, not just as congregational members.

5. Apostolic fathers provide an overall understanding of God's purposes on the earth and hear what the Spirit is saying to them as it relates to their church's mission and work.

6. Apostolic fathers provide vision and direction to their church family. They guide members of their church family to discover and fulfill God's purposes for their lives individually, corporately, and as a church to reach their city.

7. Apostolic fathers establish order and appoint spiritual leaders. These leaders help provide spiritual fatherhood and leadership to the church or churches under their care and oversight.

8. Apostolic fathers release five-fold ministry gifts to serve as spiritual fathers and mothers in God's house. They understand the vital need for them to function in the church to build up, equip God's people, and raise up God's people to full maturity.

9. Apostolic Fathers are called to raise up and reproduce themselves in spiritual sons and daughters. They are to equip, empower, and commission them as apostles or in whatever five-fold ministry office God has called them to.

REFLECTION QUESTIONS

1. How is the role and functions of a typical pastor different from the role and functions of an apostolic father? If you are in the pastoral ministry, how can you become and function more as an apostolic father? (or apostolic mother, if you're female)

2. What is the Spirit of God saying to you and your church concerning His purposes on the earth and what your church's assignment is?

3. What vision and direction are you providing your church family? How are you directing and guiding your church family corporately to reach your city?

4. How are you helping and guiding each member of your church family to discover and fulfill God's purpose for their life?

5. Do you have spiritual sons and daughters you are committed to invest your life into them and reproduce yourself in? If so, what callings do they have upon their lives? How can you effectively equip, mentor and empower them for life and the ministry God has called them to? If not, is God calling you to become a spiritual father to young apostolic sons and daughters?

A CLOSING WORD OF ENCOURAGEMENT

Let me conclude by offering a word of encouragement for first-time or young spiritual fathers. I was in Zambia last year and visited a lion park where I was able to walk with several young lions. They were a little fearful and skittish, running all over the place, unlike the full-grown lions in the park. I was amazed by the size of these young lion's paws, and I said to myself, they will soon grow into those paws to become bold, fearless strong lions. I remember when I was a young spiritual father with "big paws," I was unsure at times and a little skittish, but God was faithful to teach, equip, and mature me. I grew into the spiritual father He'd destined me to be, and so will you!

Use the principles in this book and some of the "how to's" to grow into your potential. There's no excuse for absentee, abusive, or self-serving spiritual fatherhood. You know too much to fall into that trap. Surround yourself with proven spiritual fathers and mothers who can mentor you in this divine calling and assignment.

And, may I add a word of advice to the many seasoned spiritual fathers and mothers who hold this book in their hands? You're not done. Your assignment is a life-long endeavor. Most of you have already become spiritual grandparents, and you know the blessing of raising sons and daughters, grooming them to become engaged spiritual parents who will teach, instruct, protect, direct, correct, and guide their spiritual children. There's much more work to be done, and your experience and wisdom are invaluable to God's family and the work of the Kingdom. We still need you!

To the pastors who are called to be apostolic fathers and mothers in the body of Christ, the spirit of God is *Calling You to Arise* with the Father's heart to reflect His Fatherhood and represent His image and purposes for a godly family in Christ's Church and to our communities. The fatherless are crying out and desperate to be loved, rescued, and to belong to a loving, godly family. He's calling you to adopt them, pour your life into them, and raise them up to become mature sons and daughters of God that will reflect, reveal, and do the works of Christ to transform our world.

The entire universe is standing on tiptoe,

yearning to see the unveiling of

God's *glorious* sons and daughters! Romans 8:19 (TPT)

ENDNOTES

Chapter 1

1. "The Making of a Fatherless Generation", Kenya Demographic and Health Survey, December 2018
2. OECD annual report 2014
3. Stats SA General Household Survey, 2016 - 2017
4. Fact Tank, December 2018
5. Statistics on Fatherless Children in America, May, 2019
6. U.S. Census Bureau Current Population Survey / Living Arrangements of Children Under 18, November, 2010
7. UNICEF Press Center, June 2018
8. A. Bomo, "The Fatherless Daughter Syndrome" June 2019
9. A. Bomo, "The Fatherless Daughter Syndrome: June 2019
10. A. Guerin, "The Effects of Men That Grow Up Without a Father" 2017
11. J. Mattera, "Traumatic Traits of Fatherless Men"

Chapter 2

1. See John 4:4-26 (NLT)

2. *See* Luke 15:11-24 (NLT)

3. J. Frost, *Experiencing Father's Embrace,* (Shippensburg, PA, Destiny Image, 2002)

Chapter 3

1. D. Schadt, Show Us The Father, (Lakewood, CO. Totus Tuus Press, 2016)

2. *See* Deuteronomy 6:4-6 (NIV)

3. *See* 1 John 2:12 -14 (NIV)

4. P. Wagner, *Apostles and Prophets: The Foundation of the Church,* (Gospel Light Publications, 2000)

Chapter 4

No Endnotes

Chapter 5

1. D. Wilson, Father Hunger, (Nashville, Tennessee, Thomas Nelson Publishers, 2012)

2. D. Prince, *Husbands & Fathers,* (Grand Rapids Michigan, Chosen Publishers, 2000)

Chapter 6

1. M. Hanby with C. Ervin, You Have Not Many Fathers: Recovering Generational Blessing, (Shippensburg, PA, Destiny Image Publishers, 1996)
2. M. Hanby with C. Ervin, *You Have Not Many Fathers: Recovering Generational Blessing,* (Shippensburg, PA, Destiny Image Publishers, 1996)

Chapter 7

No endnotes

For More Teaching / Ministry Resources or

To Connect with Dr. James Rene

JamesReneMinistries.com

James Rene Facebook 🅕

JamesRenePRTV Instagram 🅞

Made in the USA
Columbia, SC
27 October 2020

23591660R00098